Herkimer County
Community College Library
Herkimer, New York
13350

1. Books may be kept for three weeks and may be renewed once, except when otherwise noted.

2. Reference books, such as dictionaries and encyclopedias are to be used only in the Library.

3. A fine is charged for each day a book is not returned according to the above rule.

4. All injuries to books beyond reasonable wear and all losses shall be made good to the satisfaction of the Librarian.

5. Each borrower is held responsible for all books drawn on his card and for all fines accruing on the same.

BOOKS BEFORE FIVE

DOROTHY WHITE

Introduction by Marie M. Clay
Illustrated by Joan Smith

HEINEMANN EDUCATIONAL BOOKS
Portsmouth, New Hampshire

Heinemann Educational Books Inc.
70 Court Street, Portsmouth, New Hampshire 03801

**LONDON EDINBURGH MELBOURNE AUCKLAND
HONG KONG SINGAPORE KUALA LUMPUR
NEW DELHI IBADAN NAIROBI JOHANNESBURG
KINGSTON PORT OF SPAIN**

©N.Z.C.E.R. 1954, 1984
©Introduction to 1984 edition Marie M. Clay 1984

First Published 1954
First published in this edition 1984

ISBN 0 435 08215 9

Cover photograph by Esther Bubley, from *Esther Bubley's World of Children*, Dover Publications Inc, copyright 1981

Cover design by Ryan Cooper

Printed in the United States of America

Contents

Introduction

Books Before Five ... AFTER THIRTY YEARS

THIS is an extraordinary account of storybook reading and I am delighted to be able to recommend such a wonderful text. For many years I have encouraged parents and teachers to read it but it has been out of print for so long that copies have been hard to find even in well-stocked libraries. A new edition will be welcomed by children's librarians and parents, as well as all who are interested in the early years of childhood.

This is an intimate account told by a young mother who knew and loved children's books of how she explored her young daughter's responses to books. It begins shortly after Carol's second birthday and ends a month before she goes to school. At that time her mother wrote:

> For the last month or so Carol and I have both had a sense of standing and waiting as school beckons only four weeks away. She is like someone waiting for an adventure to begin, and I feel much as I do at a railway station performing the rites of farewell to friends going off to a larger world. (p. 189)

With images like that the author captures both the mother's, and the child's reactions as they explore the world of books, and their meanings.

I treasure the examples of child language in this book. I have quoted to many audiences of parents and teachers expressions like

'Then a tremendous excitement happened . . . ' or 'Kangaroo was born on the 95th of May', or the more serious comment that 'Not a single one of them hadn't went.' Dorothy Neal White knew a great deal about how children learn language and how important it is to develop understanding by taking time to talk about things. She knew that sharing books with a child provides opportunities for developing the intricate connections between experience, understanding, language, and eagerness to know more.

My copy of the book falls open at the quotes I have used so often. In a Little Golden Book called *Fix it Please* which I also shared with my children and remember well, there is an illustration of the father mending a chair. In the upper corner of the same page there is a small inset picture of the father's hands holding a saw and cutting a piece of wood. The child is puzzled by this:

C: Whose are those hands?
D: Those are Daddy's hands.
C: No, *those* are Daddy's hands, (pointing at full picture)
D: That's another picture of Daddy's hands, Carol.
C: Daddy hasn't got four hands. Are those Mummy's hands?
Weakly I said 'Yes,' but the riposte came quickly: 'Mummy doesn't use a saw.'
This matter was never satisfactorily settled. Two months later she was still asking about two lots of hands. (pp. 47-8)

It takes a special kind of observer to notice those exchanges with children which capture the stage of their development and how their minds are working as they try to understand each new experience. This mother accepts that understandings grow from many encounters and are the product of experience, not of being told.

The interchanges between the author and children about the world of books are so attractive. The first steps taken by one little boy are described in this quotation:

This afternoon Ann and Alan came in to play. I offered to read to them all *Millions of Cats* but Carol brought over a new Beatrix Potter, *The Tale of Mrs. Tittlemouse.* Alan, who is eighteen months old now, insisted on climbing up beside me. 'Book, book' quoth he and sat eyes wide, without a wriggle or a murmer as I talked.

Then through the range of books explored with Carol we are led to see a child in interaction with the text, the characters, the words, the pictures, the meanings, and the mother's responses.

Carol is not presented as a typical child and the books used at particular ages are not what the author would recommend to parents for other children. "What is likely to be common to all children" wrote Crawford Somerset in the Foreword, "is not the timing of certain phases of Carol's development so much as their *intrinsic nature and quality*" (my emphasis). This is not a list of books and how they went. It is an account of many exposures to new books and to old favourites, to the same book at different ages, to books that did not appeal and to those that were loved. This mother was choosing books to share with her daughter with the skill of a trained children's librarian and she looked for quality in a book.

Carol's mother's love of literature was part of the important preschool exposure of her daughter to the world of books. This is best illustrated by one episode that I like particularly.

26 MARCH 1950

Today as I stood by the stove stirring a sauce Carol said, 'Tell me some poems.' So I recited as I stirred, *John had great big waterproof boots on, Double double toil and trouble, Dr Fell, Someone came knocking,* and one or two others, until my memory for 'suitable poetry' completely failed. 'More,' the demanding voice kept saying. So I went on to

When as the rye reach to the chin
And chopcherry, chopcherry ripe within
Strawberries swimming in the cream
And schoolboys swimming in the stream,
Then, O, then, O, then, O, my true love said
Till that time come again
She could not live a maid.

"Chopcherry, chopcherry," Carol chanted. "More!" So I recited *Daffodils* and the *Ode to a Grecian urn*. "That's a long one. More!" However by now the sauce was done and the rest of the dish required all my thought.

I had the impression as I spoke that Carol would have listened to absolutely anything I said even if it had been poetry in a foreign language. It's as if she does a special kind of listening when you fix your eye on her in ancient-mariner style. Certainly it's a different kind of attention from that which she gives me when I read to her. There is a wide gulf that lies between reciting or telling aloud and reading, like the gulf between reading to one child and reading to fifty.

Alan, in the earlier example, and Carol in this one, were totally absorbed in activities which would seem to be beyond their comprehension. What is learned in such situations? The child's rapt attention tells us that *something very important is going on* although we may have to guess at what it is.

When the recorder of a child's involvement with books is a mother of such sensitivity we are sure to capture what the researcher can never describe. In her narrative this mother is always aware of the child's frame of reference, of the world of her particular experiences. She tells us of today's response to yesterday's encounter or last month's reading of a different story. This is a tale of two participants who are interpreters of their own lives, and the diary form allows us glimpses of this backward and forward flow between Carol's books and her life. Because she herself is absorbed in the child's life this mother can judge the meanings that new experiences will have for her daughter.

In 1936, as a young woman, Dorothy Neal White had won a Carnegie Travel Award and spent a year at the Carnegie Library School in Pittsburg. At that time few young New Zealanders had such opportunities for overseas travel. On her return home she was appointed Children's Librarian in the Dunedin Public Library where she launched an excellent service to schools, prepared annotated lists of books for children, wrote articles for the teacher's journal *National Education* and led the New Zealand Library Association's planning committee on school and children's libraries. In 1946 her first book, *About Books for Children*, was published jointly by the New Zealand Libraries Association and the New Zealand Council for Educational Research. The latter, a research institute, had been founded in 1933 with Carnegie funds. *Books Before Five* was published in 1954 by NZCER, this time in association with the Oxford University Press.

The year of its publication coincided with the birth of my first child. In the mid 1950s New Zealand, with its small population of 2½ million, was recovering from the war years and building towards the prosperity of the 1960s. Books and education have always been highly valued in this country and although there were not many children's librarians at that time the children's sections in public libraries were expanding. Good quality books were expensive, particularly for those with young families, so library access was very important. Libraries were well-used. Children's book publishing, which is well-established in New Zealand today, had not yet become a viable proposition so most New Zealand authors of children's books sent their manuscripts overseas to Britain or America for publication. This is the first occasion I have had reason to feel glad that New Zealand did not, in those days, publish many of its own children's books. More of our own could have meant that this book would be about stories that nobody outside New Zealand had ever heard of. As it happens this is an account of a past decade, in a distant country, but the vivid writing about an age-old story-sharing setting at or on a mother's knee (or by the kitchen sink) enables us "to think and feel our way into the very existence of children's minds."

The book is timely because it presents vividly the important role that a family plays in shaping children's opportunities to learn, exploring social relationships, and introducing them to a literate heritage through the sharing of stories. Crawford Somerset compared it to a work of art, created with the skill of an artist: "a masterly selection of significant detail from the ever-flowing stream of life".

MARIE M. CLAY

AUCKLAND

September 1984

Foreword

WHEN I opened up the manuscript of *Books Before Five* my interest was immediately aroused, and it held from the first page to the end: the book is so full of good things. One would expect this, indeed, for Dorothy White has been known to us for some years as a skilful judge of children's literature and a shrewd observer of the way children respond to what they read. And now she comes before us again, no longer as a librarian, but bringing the observations of a perceptive mother on the reactions of a very young child—her own.

Books Before Five results from a conjunction that is still uncommon in New Zealand—the trained children's librarian turned mother, who, in learning a new trade, has not lost the skills of the old. Such a conjunction is not without significance in the world of education. Mrs White's earlier work, *About Books for Children,* dealt with the books themselves, though it was shot through with penetrating glimpses into the minds of the children who read them. The present book, however, is primarily about the children (one child in particular) and the way their lives are influenced by the stories read to them in those impressionable three years before schooldays begin.

I had not read very far before I realized how little has been written about the effect of books upon the development of children in their early years. There is a vast literature on the subject of early childhood, and the student has at his disposal a wealth of observation of the way children find themselves in a world full of a number of things. We are familiar with the first random approaches to the toys of the nursery, to spoons and cups, to sand and water and the mud of the good earth, to all the stuffs and gadgets of the household, and to parents and others who move among them and give them meaning. We know something of what these things mean to the child. But the world of the child also contains books with stories for the telling. Books also bring nursery rhymes and jingles for the delight that every child feels in rhyme and rhythm. Have we given these matters the thought they deserve?

The first few pages of the manuscript had started a train of thought that persisted. There was the early mention of Adams and Henning's *First Things,* a book of pictures, 'a book fated to suffer every indignity that a child's physically expressed affection could devise—a book not only looked at but licked, sat on, slept on, and at last torn to shreds.' Here, I thought, is the first random approach to books. And 1 thought of the way children will bang a spoon on the table before they learn its use or break up a crayon before they come to respect it for the lovely marks it will make on paper. In the pages that followed there emerged very clearly the process through which Carol absorbed books into her life, and the part they played in their turn in helping her come to terms with her world.

Books Before Five is a diary, and a diary is seldom an easy thing to make a good book out of. At first glance it may easily appear to be nothing more than a medley of vivid but apparently unrelated incidents. If, as is usual, there is a fast-moving action going on in the background—political events, military operations, explorations or discoveries — this will carry the reader forward and tie the separate incidents together. When, however, the main action is the relatively slow course of human growth, day-to-day changes are seldom large enough to be perceptible, and only by skipping along the weeks can we follow that course clearly. And, naturally, the essential action of this diary is the mental growth of a child.

It would no doubt have been easier for the reader of this book to follow the threads of growth if the diary notes had been used merely as the raw material from which some psychologist had written a general study of the development of attitudes, of the changes in interest, of the widening outlook on the world, and of the enlargement of understanding that took place partly as a result of what had been read to the child. That such a study would be of value cannot be doubted; and one has only to look at the work of a Piaget to see how magnificent an edifice of generalization can be based on a very few concrete cases.

Yet the loss, in such a manner of treatment would be enormous; and this would be a pity, for there are plenty of books dealing with children's growth in general terms, but very few that give the vivid day-to-day observations from which the generalizations should emerge. Works like those of Susan Isaacs, based on her observations at the Malting House School in England, and those of Barbara Biber and her associates in the Bank Street schools in New York bring flesh-and-blood children before our eyes and enable us to think and feel our way into the very existence of other persons and give an insight that no generalized statements about human behaviour can make possible.

It has been said that an essential quality of a work of art is the way it captures and expresses something of the general meaning of things in a concrete particular example, and that by giving us a vivid image of a particular thing art enables us to see and understand its wider significance. It is not too much to say that Dorothy White's diary has this quality. The skill of the artist is seen there in a masterly selection of significant detail from the ever-flowing stream of life. And her humane under-standing of the essential quality of a child's life ensures that these fragments of existence give us a profound insight into the nature and development of children generally.

This is not the same thing as saying that the Carol of her diary is a 'typical' child and that she is growing up in a 'typical' home. Neither statement would be true. Carol is certainly a brighter-than-average child, and few homes in New Zealand are likely to give quite the same sort of entry into the world of books in general and children's books in particular as Dorothy and Dick White's. This must be taken as a warning against any over-simplified search for 'general significance' in the phenom-ena of this diary. It would be grossly wrong, for example, for anyone to say: 'Carol White began to take an interest in the meaning of . . . at three years five months, so it is high time my Janet did the same.' What is likely to be common to all children is not the timing of certain phases of Carol's develop-ment so much as their intrinsic nature and quality. The way in which a happening, such as a thunderstorm, loses its fear-inspiring quality when it can be given meaning through the the context of a story (or myth) has an essential, probably gen-eral, validity. To the student of psychology it is a very neat example of a 'redintegrated reaction' at work allaying anxiety. The particular circumstances and the particular timing of such an incident in this diary may be quite unique, but the essential experience is a universal one.

The diary is packed full of such incidents, and indeed the reader need do no more than enjoy these for the immediate and delightful glimpses they give of the mind of a child. But there is more, much more, to be got. A child is growing up in the pages of this book and the varied pattern of her social, emotional, and intellectual development gradually unfolds as the weeks and months pass. True, to perceive and to follow the many elements of this pattern is not something that can be achieved without effort on the part of the reader. Careful re-reading will almost certainly be called for, before the apparently unconnected incidents that slip by in a continuous stream begin to sort themselves out in the reader's mind, begin to group themselves around a few central themes, so that it becomes possible to see a developing design and not just a jumble of events.

At this point my natural inclination as a teacher is to show how they do, with all the enthusiasm of one who has just managed to solve an absorbing puzzle. Yet that could do a twofold disservice to Mrs White's readers: it might deprive them of the opportunity of reflecting for themselves upon the significance of episodes in the child's life, after observing them with an open mind (or at least with one unclouded by someone else's ready-made judgments); and it would certainly rob them of the fun of piecing the pattern together for themselves.

However it will not be out of place, perhaps, to offer one or two clues, by pointing out, to change the metaphor, some of the trails I have been particularly interested in following, while leaving it to the reader to spot the exact landmarks that guided me. First, there is the long path that leads to a more and more complete understanding of one's own separateness from others and yet one's relatedness to them. From the distinction between 'I' and 'we' and 'you' and 'he', the child's mind reaches out to grasp the concepts of 'mother' and 'father', 'brother' and 'sister', 'uncle' and 'aunt', neighbours and strangers and foreigners. There is, too, the gradual awareness of the fact of growth itself. Children grow up, animals grow up, 'I' grow up; a form of life begins, a form of life ends. Then 'time' itself becomes part of the mind's nature; the past and the future become objects

of wonder and questioning. And the old story of man's constant struggle to find security in the things he knows and understands and loves, while at the same time venturing forth, hesi-
tantly at first but with increasing boldness and self-reliance, to
explore the strange and court the frightening is relived in this
child's life as in every person's.

These are the great themes of life, and their introductory
phases are all to be found in the events recorded by Mrs White.
Then, passing to some of the narrower aspects of development,
we find on the intellectual side the following lines clearly
marked: a gradual understanding of the meaning of drawings
and pictorial symbols, growth in comprehending the meaning
of words, the growth of memory, the emergence of the distinction between 'real' and 'pretendy', 'true' and 'untrue'. On the
aesthetic side, too, we find a great deal of interesting material:
the joy in sounds and words, in rhymes and rhythms, and a
dawning perception of literary form not only in verse but even
in prose stories. And, of course, many phases of a child's emotional life—its joys, its fears, its likes and dislikes, its interests—
are to be found illustrated in these pages. On all such matters
the textbooks of psychology have much to tell us in a generalized manner, but here we can *see* them happening in the life of
one child.

But it is not only for the light it throws on the nature of a
growing child that this diary is significant. Equally important
is the insight we can get into the way in which external forces
impinge upon the child and influence its growth. We see indeed, a twofold process at work: in some degree Carol's way
of life determines the 'meaning' she sees in the stories read to
her; yet, on the other hand (and this is perhaps the more obvious), the 'meaning' of things as it has been revealed to her
through literature constantly influences the way she interprets

the things that happen around her. Seldom, I think, has the interaction of literature and life in these early years been so clearly portrayed. It is true, of course, that literature is only one of the many elements in our culture that influence growing children; and it is true that in this instance, because of the special interests of the parents, the stream of literature that has poured into the life of the child has been deeper and clearer than most homes can tap.

It should be remembered, too, that books were only a part, though a very important part, of the experiences of Carol's early years. An understanding of books pre-supposes contact with life outside books. This is implicit in Mrs White's diary. On this point she writes, 'the experience makes the book richer and the book enriches the personal experience even at this level. I am astonished at the early age this backward and forward flow between books and life takes place'. And Carol's life was a full one: there were the usual trips to town and to the sea, helping in the kitchen, play with the neighbours' children, the move to a new house with renovations to be done, the arrival of a new baby. It is true, on the other hand, that in this home certain aspects of cultural life received less emphasis—the natural sciences and music are examples that will readily come to mind—than they would have received in some other homes. Such qualifications, however, in no way diminish the value of the material that is presented here. The effect that literature can have on a growing child is clearly demonstrated, and we are left in no doubt about the importance of choosing good stories to read in these early years of life.

A word of caution may not be out of place at this point. Mrs White's diary should not be taken as a booklist suitable for any child in any circumstances. There are, it is true, many children's classics in the list that may well form part of the diet of most children, and that may be significant to most children for the same sorts of reasons: they may meet some common needs. On the other hand, some of the books mentioned in the diary will be quite ephemeral. Their value to one child at a given time may be very great, yet for other children in other times and other places they may have little to offer, and be not so satisfactory as others of the current publications that enter the libraries, are used up, and pass into oblivion. For different children, it would seem evident, the lists, ideally, should be somewhat different, just as their natures are different.

Parents and pre-school teachers who look to this diary to help them in their choice of stories, will find, then, no ready-made solution to their problems. What they should gain, however, is an increased awareness of the countless ways in which a child's growth towards maturity can be helped by books that do accord with the interests and needs of the varied phases of development passed through. The most practical thing about this book may be, indeed, the insight it gives into one child's mind, for through this insight we shall ourselves become more sensitive to the minds of the children in our care.

H. C. D. SOMERSET

WELLINGTON

Associate Professor of

September, 1953

The Sociology of Education

Victoria University,

Wellington

BOOKS BEFORE FIVE

1

Two to Two and a Half

SHORTLY after my daughter's second birthday I began to make some rough notes about the books that I read to her, notes which grew gradually into this reading diary, a mixture of her views and mine about the picture books we shared. Herrick looking at his daffodils has no keener sense of the passing of time than any parent looking at a child. Struck with the enormity of the idea that children grow, I began to make my record for the same reason that one puts photographs in an album, in order to remember. The photograph album gives no real record of growth, but it gives clues for the memory. So too with this diary. Unfortunately the record does not go back to the beginnings. Carol had books to look at for almost a year before this record was started, but when I came to make my notes I found that my impression of a child of eighteen months looking at pictures was vague and indistinct. By that time her first book had vanished along with lost dolls and broken feeding bottles.

That book was Adams and Henning's *First Things,* a picture book in colour photography, which was reduced to bare boards before I had noted its coming in or its going forth. In terms of this record it is prehistoric. It was a book fated to suffer every indignity that a child's physically expressed affection could devise—a book not only looked at, but licked, sat on, slept on, and at last torn into shreds. Solemn as parents are inclined to be over a firstborn, we argued gravely whether we should allow such destruction. Finally we decided, or, more accurately, drifted towards the belief that the enjoyment of personal ownership was a fact of life more worth knowing than how to look after this or that. How can one learn to hold, before one has learnt to have? So it came about that we gave Carol no advice and made no rules about the care of books until somewhere about two, when she asked me to find a picture of Simple Simon in Rojankovsky's *Tall Mother Goose*. Simon had been torn up a week before, and I explained casually that while she could tear her books if she wanted to, she must not expect the pictures to be there next time. I cannot remember her reply or subsequent actions. There are no documents in the case. From 4 February 1948, however, I kept a diary. It began with an attempt at objectivity, as a pathetic token of which I wrote the word 'child' at first, not Carol's name. I wanted if possible to achieve some sense of proportion, to keep my child and her reading in perspective. Perspective and proportion would perhaps be virtues in parents, but few of us can claim them; most of us have only curiosity and affection. The hundreds of children I had known as a children's librarian now seemed merely background figures in a tapestry of which the central figure was my own daughter. So I have written this diary as a parent, not as a librarian. So much by way of introduction. Here follows the reading record only slightly edited: some sentences have been tidied up, a few paragraphs have been transposed to give more coherence. In several places material has been omitted where it has been irrelevant or unnecessarily repetitious, or, occasionally, where it has been concerned with matters too personal to be of any general interest.

4 FEBRUARY 1948

During December and early January *My First Book* (a Little Golden Book) was gradually ousted by Rojankovsky's *Tall Book of Mother Goose*. When the child was given *My First Book* she had not seen farm animals; horses, pigs and cows were as unfamiliar to her as lions or unicorns. During early readings of the book, therefore, she passed over all the pictures of farmyard animals, but later when her 'wassat?' brought an answer, these strangers were accepted along with more familiar things. Shortly after New Year we were out with L. and he stopped the car to show our daughter some draught-horses and Jersey cows. That afternoon, too, she saw her first hens. We could not help noticing after this her increased enjoyment when she met the now known animals in her book: whereas at eighteen months she had not been interested in *any* pictures of things she hadn't seen, now at two she is willing to look at a picture of something she hasn't met in real life.

We have a steady routine with *My First Book*. Child begins by asking parent 'Wassat?' Then the process is repeated and this time the parent asks. At two years three months child identifies all the pictures with only occasional prompts. This book has some coloured illustrations, some black and white. The black and whites are often confusing to her.

We have in the house two copies of Margaret Gilmour's *Ameliaranne at the Seaside,* which have been useful when Ann from next door plays here on Thursdays. Both children revel in the many pictures of babies in these books. Even before there was a baby next door, Carol and Ann would lie on the floor looking at the pictures of babies massed on the end-papers of the book. The story as printed is of no use for telling to children about this age, but the pictures—of a bus, 'mummies in a bus', 'mummies on the sand'—make a basis for a spontaneous made-up story.

Before Christmas I began showing Carol *The Tall Book of*

Mother Goose. The appeal of the book is a quality of inexhaustibleness: its boundaries stretch so very much beyond the rim of Carol's own world. Many of the pictures, for example those of the *Queen of Hearts,* seem meaningless to the child; her face goes dull and she turns over quickly, but she is delighted by pictures of kittens, parties, 'spilt' (Miss Muffett's plate upturned), and children in a ring. Before Christmas the only rhyme she would listen to was *The House that Jack Built,* but now she recognizes and says a few words of *Three Blind Mice* (popular because of the 'specs', which both the mice and her father wear). Much of our reading time at the moment is spent just listening passively while Carol points out 'That's a boy. That's a girl. There's a mummy.'

As a librarian, I was once irritated by the constant 'mummying' and 'daddying' in the children's books in the library. Now that I have a child of my own, my sympathies—or rather my antipathies—have changed.

10 FEBRUARY 1948

Spent an hour at the children's library sorting out some books for Carol. Up till now I have relied on books she has been given; she would be quite willing at this stage to go on reading Mother Goose every night, but this palls for the parent. Even perfect love won't cast out boredom, whatever other devils it may exorcise. An important point this: parents must be considered, for if the reading becomes a chore one is too much tempted to give it up.

In choosing the books I realized how much one needed to know about the vocabulary of a little child *at the moment*. At present any book about an umbrella would be popular with Carol for she can say the word and is obsessed with the thing itself. Like the teachers I remember in my library days, I looked through the books to see what they were about; the *subject* of the narrative, not the style of its telling, had become my main consideration.

11 FEBRUARY 1948

Dick tried Dorothy Kunhardt's *Pat the Bunny* with Carol last night, and the success was so immediate that like an actor playing a 'gift' part he felt he had done it all himself. This is an American publication which is half book, half toy. It opens with a picture of two children and a statement of the

things they can do, for example, 'Judy can pat the bunny'.
Opposite these words a rabbit shape is cut out of the page and
filled in with cotton wool, a fluffy texture for a child to
touch. On other pages there is a piece of cotton to play peek-a-
boo with, a real mirror, and a ring with a hole in it to poke
a finger through. (Such books in the U.S. are called 'sensory-
perception' books I believe—the nomenclature of wonderland.)

I tried Dorothy Baruch's *Pitter Patter* in bed this morning
when Carol appeared from her room much too soon after
six a.m. The publisher's blurb gives a fair idea of this book.
'This is a book about rain. It is about the rhythm and
sound of the rain—the wonderful noises that belong to a rainy
day. Automobiles and sailboats, airplanes and animals in the
book all get wet, but the little boy, triumphant in galoshes,
raincoat, and rain hat, conquers the wetness as he sloshes
through the puddles. He stays dry.'

Struck across every page of *Pitter Patter* are the black lines
of rain; this, though it might seem a convention to an adult,
is realism to a child. The text of *Pitter Patter,* like the text of
Pat the Bunny, can be used with a two-year-old without altera-
tion. There are some repetitive texts which seem merely
boring; this one is rhythmical and satisfying, a shaped text
which on the final page reaches a climax—the little boy
under his umbrella who does *not* get wet.

The onomatopœic sound of the truck—'rumbledy rumble'
—was an enormous success. It fits in with Carol's current
mania for 'What does the pussy do?' and so on. I don't think
she associated 'pitter-patter' itself with the sound of the rain,
but she patted the aeroplane (a carry-over from last night's
Pat the Bunny). An insignia of some kind on the aeroplane's
side was hailed with delight as a brooch. Because Ann has
one, Carol is impressed with brooches and is disposed to find

them in everything. The car and the duck in the story were greeted like old friends. Much of the success of the book hinged on the fact that the elements of it were by now all familiar to Carol both by sight and by name. The climax itself did not tell with her as she has not walked often enough in the rain to discover the forbidden pleasures of puddle-stepping. On the other hand, a kindergarten student at the library the other day told me she had read the book to a group of three-year-olds at Abbotsford kindergarten, and from them there was a jubilant response when the small boy stayed dry.

14 FEBRUARY 1948

On Thursday I read *Pitter Patter* to Carol and Ann, who is just over three. They listened without stirring a muscle, the most entranced audience they have ever been. (Even at this stage of my child's reading I became aware that there was sometimes an 'extra-plus' kind of attention; with adults this occurs occasionally at a play, more often in a concert-hall.) As soon as I finished they begged, 'Do it again!' At the second reading Ann kept saying as we turned the pages, 'Will this get wet? Will this get wet?' Carol chimed in 'Rumbledy rumbledy' with the truck. The truck and the aeroplane were the favourite illustrations. To a city child an aeroplane is a fact in nature.

After this I read Esther Brann's *A Book for Baby*. As a commercial proposition this book with winsome baby face on the cover was well designed to appeal to adult purchasers round Christmas; as a proposition for reading to children it is less commendable. The text runs like this: 'Here I am. Alan Richard is my name. Here is my Mother and here is my Daddy'—a narrative use of the first person to which I should take no exception if the book were one a child could read herself. A five- or six-year-old would probably understand that the picture-child is speaking. This book, however, to judge by the age of Alan Richard and the games he played, is for children much below school age. Carol could not understand 'Here I am. Alan Richard is my name.' She only understands that when I say 'I', I mean myself; and when she says 'I', she means herself. She cannot grasp an 'I' referring to a third party, the boy in the book. Carol sees this as, 'Here is a little boy. This is his daddy.' The text of the story therefore requires a constant modification. It is, moreover, staccato and unrhythmical. I don't want fine writing or jingling rhymes, but I do enjoy the reading more, however simple it may be, when the prose has a forward-moving flow about it, the cadence which one hears in 'If it were not so I would have told you' or 'Once upon a time there were three little rabbits and their names were Flopsy, Mopsy, Cottontail and Peter.'

The Friendly Animals, by Louis Slobodkin, was a dismal failure: halfway through the first reading Carol closed the book and asked for the *Pitter Patter* book again. I had chosen the book because Slobodkin, Caldecott medal winner 'for the most distinguished American picture book for children', was an artist whose work I respected, and indeed the idea behind *The Friendly Animals* was a very good one. Slobodkin's own son when he came to have pets was led astray by the stuffed animal kingdom. In the artist's words:

These soft, completely unreliable interpretations of our animal friends left [him] unprepared to face the hard facts that real animals, even the most friendly, have teeth—claws—hoofs—horns. He was broken-hearted to learn at the age of two or three that animals do not appreciate having their tails pulled and often prove their resentment of smothering hugs of affection. . . . *The Friendly Animals* came into being as an attempt to introduce the thought to the two-to-five-year-olders . . .

that . . . animals are not an inane and decorative lot of cotton-wool and sawdust, but a healthy and independent reality.

The intentions were honourable and I honour them. But my two-year-old found the rough charcoal drawings quite incomprehensible. The pictures, not without distinction to my adult eye, were quite indistinguishable to her childish one.

22 MARCH 1948

A week ago I spent a morning at the children's library choosing new books for Carol. This morning I read Leslie Brooke's *Johnny Crow's Party* to Carol and Ann as we sat in the sun on the front doorstep. I had chosen the book because Mary had told me that Leslie Brooke's pictures were the first that her god-children had been enthusiastic about. Carol listened abstractedly for four pages, then stood up and wandered off towards the old coach-house down the garden. Ann stayed the course a little longer, when she too followed Carol off behind the rhododendrons.

In the afternoon (inside, this time) I read them Marjorie Flack's *Angus Lost,* but I found that the story needed too much adaptation for Carol at the present time. She liked the pictures of the motor car, but winter, snow, and a tethered goat were outside her experience.

24 MARCH 1948

Marjorie Flack's *Ask Mr Bear,* chosen upon a recommendation in Gesell and Ilg's *Infant and Child in the Culture of Today,* was just right for her.* This story develops from a typical childish dilemma, what to give mother on her birthday. In *Ask Mr Bear* Danny the hero, a boy of about two and a half, puts his question to the farmyard animals and receives an

---

*Arnold Gesell, Francis Ilg, and others: *Infant and Child in the Culture of Today* (New York 1943).

answer in kind; the hen suggests an egg and the cow offers milk. It is a plot of the cumulative pattern which one finds in *Henny Penny* and similar traditional stories. Each animal joins in a procession as the boy goes to the next bird or beast to get a fresh opinion. Finally he asks Mr Bear, who suggests a big bear-hug. On the first reading Carol listened with a still wrapt silence, broken only occasionally when she repeated a farmyard cackle or grunt, 'Cluck, cluck, said the hen'. During later readings she has taken a much more active part and now can hardly control her patience till we reach the bear. She begins to turn the pages over in order to reach this part as soon as possible. I have every sympathy with her. I usually jump a few chapters in a detective story to find out what happens, and with novels I nearly always make my first reading a rapid one and reserve concentration on detail for a second perusal.

The style of *Ask Mr Bear* has no particular distinction, but it is clear and well pruned. No sentences are cluttered with 'nice' and similar adjectives. Each word counts. The plot has shape and pattern, the repetition is of design—not the by-product of a flagging invention. [Later note: I read this story to her again at four years but it was past its noon. As C. said, 'When it's your birthday I'll give you a hug and a *real* present.']

25 MARCH 1948

In Margaret Brown's *A Child's Good-night Book* which Carol quickly christened her 'sleepy book', we have discovered a little classic, one with that uncloying sentiment to be found sometimes in French films. Jean Charlot's pictures reminded me a little of the work of the Douanier Rousseau and of those contemporary illustrators like Bemelmans and Ardizzone. Colin McCahon too, in his landscapes for children, has the same childlike eye on the world—the type of art of which the unadmiring say 'I could do it myself', only they never, never have.

A Child's Good-night Book opens with a double-page picture illustrating these words. 'Night is coming. Everything is going to sleep. The sun goes over to the other side of the world. Lights turn on in all the houses. It is dark'. Over the page it continues with birds, 'the little fish in the darkened sea', and rabbits and kangaroos all going to sleep. 'The sheep in the fields huddle together in a great warm blanket of wool'. As text this may seem simple enough. Indeed unless one has made one's way through second-class children's books filled with lumpy prose, one might not appreciate the quietly measured pace, the rhythmical placid style of this devisedly 'sleepy book'.

During the earlier readings of the story we did have to clamber out of some bogs of misunderstanding; for example, Carol was more than puzzled by the lions. 'Clothes-lions' is her usual pronunciation, and she looked for pegs and washing in the picture. Kangaroos baffled her too, but gradually, because these exotic animals were embedded among more familiar things, she came to accept them and give them their names when her turn came to read. When we first had the book there was a tense first listening, an immediate 'Read it again', then 'Me do it'. She was disappointed with the centre opening of the book which, because of the folding necessary in printing, was illustrated in the greyish black of the text. She wanted to waste no time with penny plain but to leap on to tuppence coloured. Distaste written all over her face, she was about to turn the page when she saw a tiny drawing of a spade which arrested her attention and gave me a chance to read the text. 'The little sailboats furl their sails and are tied up at the docks for the night. Quiet sailboats. And the cars and the trucks and the airplanes are all put in their houses in quiet garages and hangars. Their engines stop. Quiet engines.' This was the first time Carol had met a truck in books since the *Pitter Patter* book, remembering which, when we came to the truck she brought in her own descant, 'Rumbledy, rumbledy, rumbledy through the town.'

[Now reading this diary two years afterwards I find I remember with a sharp pleasure her intense happiness in that book. I am disposed to wonder however whether someone else might feel I had overestimated it. Yet one can appraise a picture book with greatest accuracy at its moment of impact.]

6 APRIL 1948

Reading experiences extend so much from day to day now that one could make a daily note if there were time. New real experiences crowd in upon Carol too, so that I wish I could go to the library more often and find books which would recapitulate the more exciting events of her life, the Sunday visits to the wharf and museum, that flea-bitten circus we saw, the new swing on the apple-tree. However, even if there are such books, I haven't always the time and energy to go to get them. Just as I find it almost easier to make clothes at home than to hunt from shop to shop, so too, much of the time I find it simpler to contrive home-made stories than to walk half a mile, catch a bus and visit the library. At the present time Carol is being fed on home-made stories. 'Carol *and* her mummy *and* her daddy went to the museum and saw fishes in a window and a chimpanzee.' 'Fishes in a window' is her circumlocution for aquarium, and we didn't bother telling her our word, not that I have anything against polysyllables for children. On the contrary, they are a sort of chutney on Monday's speech. As Beatrix Potter realized years ago, there is no need to keep a child restricted to the bare bones of language. Carol has only three polysyllables—umbrella, understand, and somersault—but these she rolls round her mouth with great satisfaction.

Yesterday it began to rain, which it has not done to Carol's knowledge for some three weeks. She looked out of the window and then began to talk about the *Pitter Patter* book, asking me to get the umbrella and put it up 'like the little boy'. In all the conversation which followed I could see the interweaving of three experiences, today's rain, the book, and an incident a month ago when we were caught in a sudden heavy shower of rain on our way back from Roslyn. She had been badly frightened by raindrops on her bare head and I had calmed her by a reference to *Pitter Patter*.

A Child's Good-night Book continues in favour. I was amused with Carol's comment 'sleepy carrot' as she pointed at a prone vegetable by a somnolent rabbit. The fish in this story are enjoying a boom as the aquarium fish at the museum, the breakfast fish, and these 'fish in the darkened sea' crowd to one point in her imagination. Last night for the first time she noticed the yellow bath mat and pointed gleefully 'fishy, fishy'.

The experience makes the book richer and the book enriches the personal experience even at this level. I am astonished at the early age this backward and forward flow between books and life takes place. With adults or older children one cannot observe it so easily, but here at this age when all a child's experiences are known and the books read are shared, when the voluble gabble which is her speech reveals all the associations, the interaction is seen very clearly. Now and again Carol mystifies me with a reference to life next door, or with some transposed pronunciation which defeats me, but on the whole I know her frame of reference.

B

The era of imaginative play has begun. This morning her doll was taken in the push-cart to the 'mus'um'. During the past week I have read Lois Lenski's *Let's Play House* to her ten or twelve times, giving a repeat performance at each sitting on the demand 'Do it again'. This is a story about three children, two dominant girls and a minor male character, who play at family life in sickness and in health. Molly and Polly feed and wash and clothe their dolls and animals, entertain guests, buy their groceries and tend the ailing.

It was noticeable a while ago that picture books with only one thing on a page had lost their appeal for Carol. This book with its more packed style of illustration follows on well. Much of the gear that Molly and Polly use in their play (dolls' feeding bottles, flour-sieves, and peg-baskets) is spread out in array as a casual border round the main subject of each picture. This, I seem to remember, is a feature of the art of some primitive people. The appeal of these borders to Ann and Carol is that they enjoy pointing out all the things not mentioned in the brief text. They label the dolls' garments with the same pleasure of an unsophisticated playgoer identifying a villain. Yet I have to admit that at first sight I thought this book was mediocre with its quite ordinary black and white pictures which do not have the aesthetic appeal of the Charlot illustrations or a book by the Petershams—I was judging it by purely adult standards.

13 APRIL 1948

I have read *Johnny Crow's Party* to her again several times but the book is never referred to in her conversations afterwards. It seems to puzzle her and she listens mazed as an adult might listen to a chant or as one might read the magic bits in Aldous Huxley's *Texts and Pretexts*.

[I was thinking of this of Peele's, quoted by Huxley.*

> *Hot sun, cool fire, tempered with sweet air,*
> *Black shade, fair nurse, shadow my white hair;*
> *Shine, sun; burn, fire; breathe, air, and ease me;*
> *Black shade, fair nurse, shroud me and please me.*]

To give her time to look at the pictures in *Johnny Crow* I have read the text slowly a line at a time and the rhyming couplets thereby lose much of their effectiveness. Carol still prefers coloured plates to line drawings, but whereas at two she could not always see that a line drawing represented anything at all, at two and a half she can make sense of a black and white sketch, even if it isn't the more glowing sense of a coloured illustration.

We are having giant trouble. Ann has a copy of *Jack and the Beanstalk*, which has either been read to Carol or told to her. Several times lately before going to sleep she has wailed miserably, 'Don't want giants. Giants go away', while I vacillate stupidly between 'No giants' and 'Giants all gone'.

Whether it is a by-product of reading or just part of the growing-up process, or the result of her experiences with animals lately I do not know, but Carol has suddenly become interested in other toys than her dolls. A rabbit, a bear and a duck, all contemporary with the dolls, have been ignored ever since she had them, but for the last weeks this zoo has been in high favour. Once or twice they have even been taken to bed in place of the formerly entrenched 'Blossom doll' and 'Debbil-doll'.

Angus Lost is now a popular book although the text still requires a little modification. Carol's experience has extended since we first looked at the story in March and the book is less

---

*Aldous Huxley. *Texts and Pretexts* (London 1935), p. 224.

alien. Now, when the days are drawing in, she sees the dark coming as the huge tangled old garden outside the window falls into shadow. The darkness sequence takes on a new meaning when she is no longer asleep before the day is really over. We have had a small snowfall, too, so she is no longer puzzled by the snow in the story. Even the incident where the dog slips out the gate means more to her since she has discovered she can open and shut the gate next door by herself. Doors and gates have become an important part of life. Pushing her dolls' cart filled with an assortment of animals between father's chair and a bookcase, she turned round to me and said, 'Just like Angus.'

About a fortnight ago she was to spend a night at the M's. I looked after Ann and Carol all day and took them both in next door about 6.45 p.m. It was the first time Carol had been outside in the dark and although I carried her in my arms in a rug she was alarmed. She screamed at first and cuddled me hard till we got inside M's gate. I remembered the instance of the *Pitter Patter* book and the rain, and said 'Look, Carol.' But before I had time she said, 'Just like the sleepy book', and indeed it was. The back of our house against the late twilight sky and the arrangement of the high English trees was an exact duplication of one of Charlot's pictures. At this point she became entranced—all terror was gone and in its place came a complete absorption in the experience. As we walked up the path she began to say little bits of the text, 'Lights go on in all the houses'.

Beth M. told me that after I had gone Carol talked about 'the dark' for a long time.

Let's Play House is now the first favourite. I hear her talking about Molly and Polly to herself and sometimes after I've read her the story she 'reads' part of the book back to me.

Doctor Peter and the not-very-well dolls have attracted some extra attention, for both Dick and I have had spells of being 'not very well' just lately. The other morning before we had a chance to describe *our* physical condition Carol came in and announced 'I'm not very well. Doctor Peter come'.

We still read *The Tall Book of Mother Goose* with *Three Little Kittens* as favourite. I get constant demands all day to tell her this one, and milk drinking is speedier if kittens are dangled as bait. She can now repeat in garbled fashion *Boy Blue, Humpty Dumpty*, and *Jack and Jill*. Most of the time these days she is absorbed in her own busyness. A doll's swing suspended on her cot kept her quiet for an entire morning. Beds for dolls are made in every available box and even those which are not available are liberated. She washes clothes for an hour at a time while she and the bathroom floor grow sodden.

Jean de Brunhoff's *Babar the King* has been popular as a book of pictures. Some of the illustrations are meaningless to a very small child but others, the camels with 'parcels on their backs', the picture of the elephant city with each elephant gazing from his respective window, and the elephants making a garden ('like Keith,' says Carol)—all these she likes. There is one sequence of two pictures in which Zephyr the monkey falls into a bowl of pudding. I hadn't explained this to Carol as we turned over the pages, but to my surprise I found that this action fragment of the picture appealed to her instantly. 'Monkey get all wet.' Now she turns to it almost at once. Two other pictures she likes are one of the young elephants in kindergarten and another of their elders at the opera. When we are going out now Carol assumes we are going to a concert, for in this, as in much else, the language in use next door is the one which Carol adopts in preference to our own. What boots it that we say bed, or living-room, if we describe our evenings out as 'going to talk to people'. Next door they say 'byes' and 'dining-room', and they go to concerts. Carol under the spell of the M's insists we are going to a concert every time we dress to go out. Thus the opera picture intrigues her because she imagines she has a view of life with father and mother.

21 MAY 1948

'Just like' is a phrase much in vogue at the moment. I have begun to use the sewing machine when Carol is about as she is old enough now not to be an unmitigated nuisance when I am dressmaking. Yesterday I went out of the room to answer the telephone and I came back to find Carol sitting at the machine. She looked up with a grin 'Just like Molly and Polly'.

Ask Mr Bear has also passed into her speech. For a month or so she has been giving me big bear-hugs. Yesterday she asked for a 'whisker'. I didn't understand at first till I realized from something else she said that this was more from the 'bear book'. She wanted a whisper in her mother's ear like her hero Danny.

2

Two and a Half to Three

Now two and a half, Carol finds pictures everywhere, some of them pictures so small that they are overlooked by an adult eye until a child's pointing finger brings them into focus. Here is a soldier on a matchbox lid, there on the packet of razor blades is a man's head. To be in the house with her just now is a perpetual process of re-discovering one's own environment. Outside the house I notice this even more. As we walk up Garfield Avenue I share with her a new world around my own feet, the dandelions by the gutter, a piece of blue glass on the footpath, sparrows' droppings, locks on gates. All this for her, as Walden for Thoreau is 'pasture enough' for the imagination. At home again, true to her femininity, she will pore over the pages of *Vogue* or *Harper's Bazaar*, seeing the 'ladies'—ladies, ladies, everywhere; never, I notice, 'mummies'. We have in the hall a medieval print, blue and gilded, which R.E.R. gave to me when she was born. Like the nurse who stared at this picture in the maternity home ('Great what they get up to nowadays!') Carol stares too, perplexed by the mythical sea where a mermaid fingers a lute and five carps and dolphins rise from the water with trumpets in their mouths. 'Fishies playing tunes,' she says.

Recently several books I have brought home from the library have been markedly unsuccessful and without appeal to her. Like other parents Dick and I became enchanted with some books and could not wait to share them with our child —or perhaps rather less altruistically we wanted like Stevenson 'to indulge the pleasure of our own hearts'. Thus I brought home Golden MacDonald's *Little Island,* the Caldecott medal winner illustrated by Leonard Weisgard. Carol had shown some interest in the island off the coast at St Clair, but I do not think she could connect that blob in the middle of the sea with the island in the MacDonald book. Nor did she appear to connect the pictures with one another. They remained isolated, and were not a series or a sequence to her. Marjorie Flack's *Tim Tadpole and the Great Bull-frog* also proved too foreign. A country child who had played by water-race or river back-water might have liked the book, but Carol has urban limitations of outlook.

Tammy and That Puppy by Dorothy and Marguerite Bryan failed for rather different reasons. This is the story of a Scotch terrier who is upset when a small pup is added to the family, a statement in canine terms of an older child's feelings when a new baby is born. The book might be useful in that situation. For a story of its size, thirty pages and perhaps twice as many sentences, *Tammy and That Puppy* was like the opening chapters of some Russian novels somewhat overloaded with characters—five human beings and five dogs. Carol and Ann had difficulty in distinguishing dog from dog. A d'Aulaire picture book, *Too Big,* did not interest her either. This is the story of a little boy who has grown too big to get into last summer's clothes, an experience which has happened to Carol in the sense that it has occurred, but not in the sense that she is aware of it. *Too Big* was quickly returned to the library, and with it went *Don't Count Your Chickens* by the same authors. The plot of the latter book develops around a peasant woman's dreams of what she will buy with her egg-money —more animals, a suitor, a bigger farm. These hopes are smashed when the eggs drop from her basket. Now this theme of ruined hopes and unsubstantial castles in the air is a familiar one in the folk-tales read and appreciated by eight- and nine-year-old children, but it is more truly an adult theme. When, as with a two- or a three- or even a four-year-old, the gulf between possible and impossible is not discerned, such a story loses its point. The woman is not ridiculous for having high hopes; and to complicate matters further Carol believed that the woman's dreams had materialized, because the illustrations show the things she hopes for.

For a very young child a picture of a thing establishes the existence of that thing. To vary the philosopher's statement, 'It is in a picture therefore it is'. Carol thought the woman in *Don't Count Your Chickens* had got her new farm. I remember that Constance told me once of her difficulties when she read Margery Bianco's *Franzi and Gizi* to her daughter. In this tale the girl Gizi imagines that her grandmother is dead, and the relevant pictures show her crying by a grave. Later in the story the same grandmother's preparations for an evening meal are mentioned. 'But she's dead,' said Constance's daughter, 'She is dead.' Nothing would move her. The same point was underlined for me again when I read Carol *The Indoor Noisy Book* which concludes with a series of questions: 'Who is coming up the stairs? Is it a sailor? Is it a soldier?' I read the answers: 'No, it isn't a sailor. No, it isn't a soldier.' Yet

as the illustrations show a sailor and a soldier Carol contra-
dicts me. 'Yes it is. There he is.' Marjorie Flack was so much
wiser in a similar set of questions at the conclusion of *Ask
Mr Bear*. Guessing what her birthday present will be, Danny's
mother asks, 'Is it a pillow? Is it an egg?' Here there are no
illustrations of purely imaginary things.

Linked with this is a secondary matter. If for a child what
is in a picture is, likewise, what is not in a picture is not.
In the d'Aulaire *Too Big* the boy is shown holding to mother's
apron strings, but mother stops at the waist. 'Where is that
mummy's head?' Ann demanded of her mother. Any explanations were useless. Ann was convinced that the mother was
decapitated. In this example the picture stopped, but Carol
is also worried sometimes when an object is half hidden behind
another object in the picture itself. She was puzzled over
pictures in *Linsey Woolsey* where Tom goes swimming in the
river and Sylvie peers at him from behind a tree. 'Where
are the little boy's legs?' I explained that they were hidden
in the water. 'But where are they?' She pressed the paper as
if to find them. No metaphysician propounding theories of
being could feel more frustrated by language than I do in
explaining all this.

30 JUNE 1948

I am reading Marjorie Flack's *Angus and the Cat*, although
it requires some adaptation. The preliminary pages about
Angus learning things, for example that balloons go pop and
frogs jump, have nothing much to do with the rest of the
story. The frog is introduced with a picture and then is heard
of no more. Perhaps this is cavilling: anyway irrelevant or
not, the balloon was appreciated. When Dick took the book
in to Carol to-night she went 'Pop, pop' before he had a

chance to begin. Generally speaking the book is well contrived. In contrast with the ten characters of *Tammy and That
Puppy,* here in the main part of *Angus and the Cat* there are
only two, the Scotch terrier and puss. No confusion can possibly
arise. There is a limit to the number of characters Ann and
Carol can think about at the same time. Although *Ask Mr Bear*
had a largish cast, these were all very different animals who
had their say then merged into the procession behind the hero.
Only one at a time shared the centre of the stage with Danny.
In that book and in *Angus and the Cat* where the child also has
to concentrate on two animals only, one sees how Marjorie
Flack understands so well the limits of the young listener's
understanding. (Something of the same thing is true of the
comic-strip artist.) Miss Flack always makes sure there will be
no misunderstanding. At the end of her story Angus is looking
for the cat. 'He looked on the sofa—no cat was there. He
looked on the mantel—no cat was there. Angus looked on
the table—no cat was there!' No child can possibly forget
what Angus is searching for. Moreover the sofa, the mantel,
and the table have all been illustrated previously as haunts of
the cat—the stage has been set, the background created in a
substantial way before the main action takes place.

26 JUNE 1948

This morning I read Beatrix Potter's *Tale of Tom Kitten* to
Carol. After a series of failures and near failures in choosing
stories lately I was happy to see something hit the target.
Here were kittens tumbling about a doorstep in the dust,
much as she likes to do herself where the gravel is wearing
thin. Mrs Tabitha Twitchitt expects friends to tea. Mittens,
Tom Kitten, and Moppet are to be washed, combed, and given
clean clothes. Here for Carol was a comprehensible universe.

Carol was only mildly interested when the kittens dirtied their clothes. I usually find that small children are very happy to say 'Naughty' to some miscreant in a story. Thus Carol was quick to apply the label 'Naughty' both to the monkey in *Babar* who falls in the pudding and to the cat in *Let's Play House* who jumps out of a doll's pram where he is supposed to act as a docile baby. However, because in her moral calendar the soiling of clothes is no evil she made no such judgment on the dirty kittens.

The entry of the ducks, 'pit, pat, waddle, pat' down the high road, was enjoyed, but when Mrs Tabitha Twitchitt finds her kittens on the wall bare of clothes after the ducks have absconded with them, Carol did not appear to get the point. After all, the kittens looked much the same as the Garfield cats disporting themselves on the rockery.

2 JULY 1948

We have read *Tom Kitten* together four or five times. When I look back to notes taken only a week ago, I can see how much more Carol is getting from the story since she has become more familiar with it. Although I have always felt one shouldn't tamper with a Beatrix Potter text I find myself doing so, and inserting our expressions instead of some of Beatrix Potter's more Edwardian ones. Thus I changed 'fine company' to 'friends' and replaced 'while she made hot buttered toast' with 'getting the afternoon tea ready'. We do not eat toast in the afternoon. Meantime Dick has read the real version. Today Carol drew me up with a reproach —'No, no.' I returned to 'hot buttered toast'. When Tom's mother sews on his buttons Carol prompted me with an explanation I had made one day and forgotten the next—'When my buttons come off my Mummy sews them on again.' One needs the

memory of an elephant if one is going to adapt at all. Now
at the fourth reading she is starting to tell the story to me.
'He scratched,' she says, pointing at Tom Kitten. She wants
to hasten to the end of the story which by now has become
a real climax. The pictures of kittens wrecking their bedroom

did not interest her until I explained that they were pulling
all the clothes out of the drawers. This made naughtiness of
a recognizable kind. Wickedness has to be in scale to be
appreciated.

Today too she was enthusiastic about the pictures of the
kittens being spanked, and asked to have it again. As I realized
today when her cold developed, she has been out of sorts
and I have been short-tempered. I smacked her yesterday,

hence the interest. This afternoon she came to my room to play while I rested. I suggested she could play 'Tom Kitten' with my chest of drawers—at least it kept her from crawling over my bed. For quite an hour this game of pulling out and putting back amused her. Then she was back at my side with a 'dinner ready' of buttons and beads in an old cigar box.

3 JULY 1948

Carol is fretful with her cold. I tried Beatrix Potter's *Benjamin Bunny* but the plot was too elaborate. *Peter Rabbit* however proved as successful as *Tom Kitten*. Here again was a situation that was familiar (in the social sense). 'They all lived with their mother at the root of a very big fir-tree'. Mother gives her instructions and goes off shopping. Peter Rabbit crawls under the gate to the world of Mr McGregor's garden and a literary reputation. Under the gate and out, Peter had Carol's sympathy from the beginning. The shoe lost among the cabbages, the jump into the watering can, the mouse by the door, all the detailed perfection of this story charmed her, although we had one or two stumbles. The second watering-can picture where only Peter's ears protrude worried her. 'Where is the rest of him?'

This story is much longer than any she has had before and although she asked me to read it again I saw that towards the end of the second reading her attention wandered.

[*Peter Rabbit* was read two or three times a week during the next few months and became in our family as in thousands of others a classic bedtime story. So much so that in the diary I seem to have taken it for granted like hair washing or the Sunday walks. At all events there are no notes of any length about it until October during a visit to Christchurch and again on our return in November. These are given out of order for the sake of coherence.

OCTOBER-NOVEMBER 1948

The incident of the goldfish pool in *Peter Rabbit* did not interest Carol very much until after she had visited her cousins and seen their pond and fountain and fish. After that she began to touch the picture to examine every detail in it.

The opening part, where Mrs Rabbit takes her umbrella and basket and goes to the baker to buy buns, has stirred Carol to the depths. She is forever talking about the buying of buns (food which in fact we never purchase) and every time an umbrella is dropped in the hall Carol takes it, finds a basket, and informs me that she is off to the baker's.

The herbal lore of the rabbits has also been adopted. She was asking for camomile tea in Christchurch and was enraged when at first I couldn't understand what she was asking for in a proffered cup. 'And then feeling rather sick he went to look for some parsley.' Carol occasionally announces an indisposition: 'My tummy's sore. I want some parsley.' I don't have to provide the parsley on these occasions. The 'I want' isn't one of those 'have-to-be-met' demands like 'I want my nose blown!' but is quite conscious play. She has always liked to peer at the shoe lost amongst the cabbages but a week ago or so when we came to the rest of the sentence, '. . . and the other shoe amongst the potatoes', she was not satisfied with a verbal statement alone; she wanted a picture. 'Where is the shoe among the potatoes? Where are the potatoes?']

20 JULY 1948

Both Carol and Ann are enjoying *Toby's House,* by Lois Maloy. 'This is Toby's house. This is Toby. This is a chipmunk. "Where do you live chipmunk?" says Toby. "I live on my stone wall," says the chipmunk.' Toby asks the duck, the butterfly, the spider, the rabbit, and the frog, and he discovers that all the animals have their places to live. The climax comes when the little boy finds a homeless dog which he takes to his own house for supper and bed.

The first time that I read the story to the children they listened quietly, but on the second reading fingers were pointing, questions were asked. They liked a tiny detail, Toby looking out of the window of his house. 'I like *that* butterfly,' said Carol, distinguishing it from the flies and bees about Garfield Avenue, which she always insists are butterflies. They were doubtful about the frog and the spider's web, but the rabbit received an ovation; each child insisted on patting and kissing the page. The beehive intrigued them, also Toby's bee-keeper's hat. 'Why is the bee in the flower?' asked Carol. I explained about making honey and taking it home to the hive, but they both looked rather doubting.

Towards the end of the book I stumbled on a misconception they both had had. In one illustration Toby and his dog have dinner, while over the page Toby and his dog are shown near a bed. 'Is that little dog going to have dinner?' asked Ann. I don't remember their other remarks, but these caused me to wonder to what extent the children realized that the pictures in books are consecutive. I remembered similar difficulties when I came to read *Tammy and That Puppy* and a few months ago after reading *A Book for Baby* I had noted that Ann did not understand that a sequence of four action pictures represented the same thing. She said 'Four horses.'

The end-piece of the book, Toby's house in darkness, provoked much talking as we sat together on the sofa. Carol is full of memories of 'the sleepy book', and often in the evening shows me 'the dark' in the bushes. In the picture book I showed them stars and moon, and Carol repeated my information to Ann.

Two weeks ago I read her the *Story of Babar,* actually the first of the series, although she was told *Babar the King* some months ago. I couldn't bring myself to kill the mother elephant so I sent her to hospital. 'Where's the "hostipal"?' she asked. Most of all she liked the shopping sequence and riding in the lift, because it so happened that on this particular morning we had been to town and taken two rides on a lift ourselves. The photograph of Babar pleased her but she didn't understand about the camera. Over and over again I see that her reading enjoyment is contingent upon the range of her previous experience.

12 SEPTEMBER 1948

During these early spring months there has been a considerable tapering off in the amount of reading we've done. Went to Wellington for a week in August and Carol again stayed with Ann. The weather has been fine and we have been out shopping together much more than usual. Her activities have increased in number, and scope, and duration. 'Cuttings out' are in fashion and the construction toy we call 'the building town' occupies much of her day. Here and next door she and Ann will spend a whole afternoon cooking with dried cereals and grey bits of pastry on a box. Carol is always busy and books have played a very small part in her life. Homemade stories, little more than elaborate explanations really, are much more to her taste. J., a bride of three months, brought her husband to see us and stayed here overnight while he went on to Invercargill. Here was a new type, a husband; but 'Where are your little boys and girls?' I explained about wives and husbands, sons and daughters, mothers and fathers. (One could hear the whirr of Miss Compton-Burnett's wings.) We went through all the people we knew, classifying them according to status. 'Keith is a husband, Alan's a son, Malcolm's a son,' I would say. Next day, 'Mummy talk.' 'What about?' 'Husbands.' On we'd go.

28 SEPTEMBER 1948

Carol began kindergarten on 14 September. The stories she hears there are seldom mentioned in her conversation, although at the present time when she has experiences I do not share it is much more difficult to follow her allusions. One morning last week I called early at the kindergarten and found Miss D. reading a group of three-year-olds *Little Red Riding Hood*. This explains Carol's talk about eating people.

1 OCTOBER 1948

The 'Toby book', *Toby's House,* continues in favour. She is happy to look at it in bed night after night. I have also read her Tasha Tudor's *Linsey Woolsey* again. This is a period story set in mid-nineteenth century New England, its characters children in long dresses and pantaloons, a style of dress on which Carol makes no comment. The book has a format similar to a Beatrix Potter story and something of the same flavour, the same well-loved cottage interiors and pastel landscapes. Like Beatrix Potter, Tasha Tudor tells her tale with unselfconscious seriousness: there is no adaptation of vocabulary to suit a little child's ear. I made one or two adjustments when I first read the book to Carol some time ago but lately I have gone ahead and read the book as written. Words like 'indignant', 'curiosity', and 'unbearable' seem to explain themselves in the context. Carol was completely absorbed by the story when I read it to her yesterday after a lapse of some weeks. She has looked at the book a great deal by herself and after I finished reading yesterday she began to show me the pictures she liked most, notably Tom and Sylvie churning ice-cream.

Sylvie Anne in this story has a birthday party but Linsey Woolsey, a mischievous lamb, spoils the proceedings. He breaks away from a post where he is tethered, something

Carol is now able to comprehend since she has seen the tethered bulldog at Mrs N's so often on Sunday walks, and has read about it again in one of the Angus books.

[*Linsey Woolsey* was read again to Carol in November after her own birthday party with a to-be-expected heightened response. At the beginning of December 1948 it was returned to the library and she has not seen it again. Here I must interpolate two entries from my journal a year later, two months after we had moved to another house.

27 NOVEMBER 1949

This morning I was hanging out clothes and Carol said, 'I wish I had that lamb book.' Helpfully I recited 'Mary had a little lamb', but she looked cross and said, 'No, the library book I mean.' The nursery rhymes are her own property, so I knew that guess was wrong. She returned to the pursuit. 'Not Mary. You know, the other one, the lamb on the table.' I could recall no such animal and racked my brains. Carol, who always examines my face intently, was seething at my obvious bewilderment. If I don't understand an allusion she almost dances with rage. 'Mummy, the lamb on a table at a party.' Suddenly it came to me. 'You mean *Linsey Woolsey*.' The jerking little figure rested and was calm. 'That one, that library book, I wish I could have it.'

8 DECEMBER 1949

This morning I looked out of the window at Carol's dresses blowing in the wind in the back-garden, and I saw that something in the scene, the effect of light and movement did recall the picture of the lamb and the table in *Linsey Woolsey*. That patch of garden by the clothes line, with its poppies, granny-bonnets, and honesty, a cottage garden really, is in its colours like the pastel shades Tasha Tudor used in her water-colours. The washing blowing in the wind did remind me of the movement and confusion of Sylvie Anne's party when the lamb climbed up to upset her birthday party. I would not have thought of comparing the two but for Carol's remarks a few days ago. Anyway, something there in the garden did remind her of the book she had been read over a year before.]

12 OCTOBER 1948

Last time we were at the library, Carol poked about among the bookshelves and came up triumphant with Esther Brann's *A Book for Baby* which she had been read earlier in the year. Looking back to my notes I find I was not at all enthusiastic about the book then. Now I have to recant. Carol has been picking this one up and looking at it by herself more often than any other book. She doesn't ask me to read it, but just sits and stares at the pictures, particularly at a set of four showing a gang of small children at play with trucks and motor-cars. The illustration reminded me, and probably reminds Carol too, of the Saturday mornings when Ann, Carol, Raymond, John, Margaret, and Leonie play out on the lawn here.

We also borrowed *Angus Lost* from the library again, another book that in March was beyond her understanding and is now, in its text at least, quite suitable. The pictures however still present a problem or two, notably the milkman who is cut off at the waist, and a big car shown receding in the distance. 'But that's only a little car.'

She is tremendously involved in a story like this and her comments make a secondary story in themselves. 'What's the pussy doing on top of the gate?' 'Where's Angus' mummy?' 'What's his mummy's name?' Everything these days must have a house and a mummy. I read her *A Child's Good-night Book* the other evening and when we came to the part about 'the sun going over to the other side of the world' she asked, 'Where's the darkness house? What's the darkness mummy's name?'

30 OCTOBER 1948

On October 14 I took Carol up to Christchurch to see my family, the first visit since she was a year old. I took *Peter Rabbit* up in the train to read and we had one look at it during the late morning. Most of the journey however she looked out of the window, an absorbed spectator, eyeing the landscape to discover cows and sheep. Rivers, harbours, boats, and livestock were her main interest—I suspect she found landscape without animals a little boring.

When we arrived in Christchurch, Carol was delighted to find her cousin Virginia there too. For the three days before Virginia left she and Carol withdrew from the adults altogether and played in the garden from morning till night. How infinitely less exhausting two children are than one!

Looking back on it, I can see what an enormous extension of Carol's experience this was, particularly the discovery of grandparents, aunts, uncles, and cousins—'real relations' like Ann's. I hadn't known, until she made the comparison, that she had been very much aware of Ann's larger circle, that she had in fact missed having aunts and grandparents about.

3

Three to Three and a Half

FROM eight o'clock this morning Carol followed me round
the house with a duster and her toy broom and carpet
sweeper, copying my every movement until by eleven o'clock
the mimic housekeeper was as tired as the real one. When
I suggested a story she went to her room and returned with
one of the Ameliaranne books, *Toby's House,* and *The Tale
of the Flopsy Bunnies.* I seem to remember trying this sequel
to *Benjamin Bunny* earlier in the year and finding the plot too
difficult. This morning Carol insisted upon the book, and tired
as she was there seemed little point in having an argument on
the matter. The plot, as I had half remembered, proved a
complicated one. The Flopsy Bunnies fall asleep after eating
the lettuces on a rubbish pile. ('It is said that the effect of
eating too much lettuce is soporific,' says Miss Potter in a
now famous aside.) When McGregor comes to empty his
lawn mowings on the pile he finds six sleeping rabbits which
he drops into a sack to be taken home later for dinner. In

this predicament the Flopsy Bunnies are discovered by Mr and Mrs Benjamin B. who enlist the aid of a mouse to chew a hole in the sack. On their release the captives refill McGregor's sack with rubbish, and the story ends with the discomfiture of Mr and Mrs McGregor, who realize they have been hood-winked. Instead of rabbits, there are only 'three rotten vegetable marrows, an old blacking brush and two decayed turnips'. The details are pure Potter.

To all this Carol listened with a puzzled frown, obviously baffled but not bored. She listened to the end and as I read piled questions one on top of the other in an attempt to understand it. 'What's that?' 'Lettuces.' 'Are the little rabbits eating them? Why are they eating them?' She asked questions too, about the mouse chewing a hole in the sack as she could not understand (nor could I) why the rabbits couldn't chew the bag for themselves. English 'lawn mowings' had to be translated into New Zealand 'grass clippings', and we suffered another attack of our old trouble with 'decapitated' pictures when McGregor is represented by his boots alone.

The end of the story, where the rabbits watch the final discomfiture of McGregor, fell quite flat. Such an incident, when an audience 'in the know' watches the tumbled hopes of a character, is a stock device in traditional comedy, but the device is only successful if one is simultaneously aware of the two themes which make the contrast and if one can withhold sympathy from the befooled one. All this Carol cannot do. She can only think of one thing at once and consequently became sorry for McGregor. 'Poor Mr McGregor, he won't have any dinner.' She did not see that if he had had rabbit for dinner it would be a case of 'Poor Flopsy Bunnies'.

A further difficulty arose when an illustration showed

McGregor's hands putting the rabbits in the sack. The text reads, 'The Flopsy Bunnies dreamt that their mother was turning them over in bed. They stirred a little in their sleep but they did not wake up.' I don't think Carol could understand rabbits who think one thing is happening to them while something different actually occurs.

When we had finished *Flopsy Bunnies* she did not ask for the story again but said, 'Now this one,' pointing to *Ameliaranne's Prize Packet* by Eleanor Farjeon, a bedtime book which she usually 'reads' by herself. Before we went for the Christchurch holiday Carol suddenly began to tear books when there was no supervision. I made a habit of giving her this book in bed, so that she could concentrate her damage there, a sort of whipping boy. The text of this book is intended for seven-year-olds but the illustrations make a useful basis for my own made-up stories. Pictures show Ameliaranne looking in the windows of a village toyshop and for these Carol's enthusiasm is boundless; a doll in a pink dress is an enchantment. 'Can I have one like that for my next birthday? A little pink dress *and* a white hat *and* little shoes.'

After *Ameliaranne* she wanted *Toby's House*. Before making these notes I turned back in my diary to 20 July where I had made a full record of one of the dozens of readings we have had of this story during the year. Comparing those notes with this morning's reading I can see how much less animated and less questioning Carol was today. *Toby's House* is by now much easier for her to understand than the other two books read this morning, which had both required in one way or another some intellectual effort. With them she had to grapple with much that was unfamiliar, with Toby she was happy resting and listening without interruption to the simple pattern of a familiar story.

15 NOVEMBER 1948

By now after a year's hard wear, the Rojankovsky *Tall Mother Goose* has lost its cover and many pages. These nursery rhymes run in cycles of popularity with Carol. For a long time *Willie Winkie* was her favourite but he now is superseded by *Hey Diddle Diddle, Little Boy Blue, Simple Simon, Sing a Song of Sixpence,* and *The Old Woman Who Lived in a Shoe.* All the Mother Goose characters are more than jingles to her; they represent a world which overflows into her own just as Dickens characters do with a Boz enthusiast. Thus *Simple Simon* seems connected in her mind with the fishermen she sees on the Sunday walks to the wharves: if she has eaten bread into a funny shape she will say, 'Look, there's the old woman's shoe.'

I find that the stories she is told at kindergarten are rarely referred to in her conversation, or at least are not referred to in a form which I can recognize. Most of her talk about kindergarten centres round the individual children she meets there—A. who goes with his grandmother, B. who hits, C. who is allowed to have sweets, D. with a pretty blue hat, and E. who won't wait for F. at lunch-time. All this life with many other children has resulted in her obsession with names, and now when we read a story or look at pictures in a magazine everyone in a group has to be named. 'Who's that?' 'A man, a woman, a girl'—such answers will not do. 'What's her name?' Carol persists. Sometimes imaginary names will do but at other times where a picture shows children of her own age I have to label the group with the names of the children she plays with—Margaret, Leonie, Annette and Peter. Any omissions are corrected and reproved. 'Where's Alan? You haven't said Alan.'

Some form of religious education is given at the kindergarten during the first period of the morning when the youngest children share lessons with the rest of the junior school. This I think is followed by half an hour of games and singing round the piano. The two experiences seem to telescope in Carol's mind. I hear her talking about Jesus, but it is a Jesus of her own contriving, whose name usually appears in those stories she makes up which have a background of Mother Goose lore. I remember one such—'Jesus arms round me went to the Hubbard.' Another probable by-product of all this has been the appearance of an imaginary playmate she shares with Ann, one Jeejer, whose name may be a portmanteau word from teacher and Jesus.

Last week when Leonie (five) came round for the afternoon I read them both Lois Lenski's *The Little Family*. On Carol's command the two 'cuddled up for stories'. My daughter gives an almost ritualistic wriggle into place before I begin. A note on the back of the title page reads: 'This book was made for S.C. who is three', and the text is simplicity itself. 'Here is the Little family. Mr and Mrs Little and Sally and Tommy Little. The Littles live in a little house. It has doors and windows and a chimney on top. . . . Mrs Little sweeps the floor. Sally helps her mother. . . . Mrs Little goes to market. She carries a basket. Tom and Sally go with her. Mrs Little buys sugar, bread, carrots, oranges and other things. She pays money for them.'

While I read this elementary narrative Leonie and Carol sat like mice, enjoying every word. The book held nothing that was beyond their experience, and it seemed to me that their absorption in such a story which confirms rather than extends experience was rather similar to Carol's present response to *Toby's House*. That book originally contained material from beyond her environment but by now this has been so thoroughly absorbed that it almost counts as personal experience. Even at this age there can come a stage when the literary experience has almost an equivalent reality to the actual. The point which interests me here is how one should assess the comparative value of *The Little Family* and *Peter Rabbit*. I suspect that a child has a need both for the book which 'merely' confirms, like *The Little Family,* and for the book like *Peter Rabbit* which extends beyond the immediately known. In one of her essays* Rebecca West says, 'This use of art to prove what man already knows is a shameful betrayal of the mission of art to tell more than he knows.' This may apply to adult literature but it does not apply to children's literature at the beginning. In fact one could argue that they have a need for literature which tells them what they already know. Indeed I am not convinced that even an adult will accept the validity of a literature which does not confirm his own experience if he has not previously appreciated some writing to which he said, 'This is I.'

22 NOVEMBER 1948

At John's farewell party I fell into conversation with Dietrich about our children and their books. The Becker family favourite is Lear, which Sandra has enjoyed since she was eighteen months, particularly *The Owl and the Pussy Cat*.

This talk spurred me on to another attempt to interest Carol in *Nonsense Songs* but I have been no more successful than before. Why, I don't know. She may be a practically minded child with 'no nonsense about her', or on the other hand her distaste may come from the fact that she has heard very little spoken to her that has been quite incomprehensible. It is as though she expects words to mean something in an obvious and substantial way as some legally trained men and

*'Charlotte Brontë', in *Great Victorians*, Vol. I (Pelican Books, 1937), p. 75.

scientists do. When I began *The Owl and the Pussy Cat* she barely listened but kept interrupting to ask about the pictures. 'Why is the pussy's tail like that?' When I had finished one verse she put her hand over the page and then began to turn over the leaves. Next I tried the *Jumblies* of which she tolerated two verses before she closed the book firmly and said, 'We'll have this one now.'

'This' was another Lois Lenski, *Spring Is Here,* which proved most disappointing after *Let's Play House*, by the same author. The text, which told no real story and bore little relationship to the pictures, was of an ejaculatory gunshot kind. 'Spring is here today. Open the door. Come out and play. Spring has come to stay.' There were some gardening pictures which might have been interesting if the boy and girl in them had been given names and a real identity for a listening child, but their activities in the garden were vaguely and not precisely described. Carol now likes a book in which details are pin-pricked home.

Over the last month or so Carol has begun to tell me stories. These are always told with a change of tone from her natural way of speaking, for like some clergymen and radio speakers she uses a ritual voice. This one she 'read' to me from an old alphabet book. 'Once upon a time'—pause—'Jesus' mummy said we are going to have a party, and that's Leonie G. and that's Ann M. and I'm Carol White, 17 Garfield Avenue.'

16 DECEMBER 1948

There was no outstanding success among the library books I chose early this month. *The Little Fireman* went back un-opened, for on second thoughts it seemed early to interest Carol in burning houses. *This is the Milk that Jack Drank,* a modern adaptation of Mother Goose which attempts to give the old lady some social significance, proved on trial a complete failure with both Ann and Carol, who ran off the minute I had finished this revised version. They like the original *House that Jack Built,* but this new didactic Jack had none of the

cheerful forward march of the old one. The real trouble I suspect lay in the subject of *This is the Milk that Jack Drank.* The milk that Carol and Ann drink is strictly a bottle product which appears on doorsteps long before they are even awake, and it has no history.

Because the train journey to Christchurch was a big event in Carol's life I borrowed from the library two books about trains, *The Northbound Express* by Aileen Findlay and Rona Dyer, a book written, illustrated, and published in Dunedin, and *The Story of the Little Red Engine* an English publication by Diana Ross. The staff of the children's library have told me that *The Northbound Express* has been an exceptionally popular book with Dunedin children in the primers and early standards; it is a book, one of the very few that New Zealand children ever see, which describes their corner of the world. However with my two its success was only partial. So much of this train journey is seen by the artist as from a point far beyond the train, as an observer in an aeroplane or a country child watching from a hill-top might view an express. This distant vantage point of vision produces some of Rona Dyer's best pictures but Ann and Carol responded most to the earlier, 'less artistic' drawings of a railway siding, refreshment room, and carriage interior—all this is what they think of as a ride in a train. [It is the virtue of Helen and Margaret Binyon's *Railway Journey* published shortly afterwards that their book preserved the child's eye view of train travel, for in that book the pictures might have been drawn by someone two feet away from the boys in the story. Beatrix Potter, too, also keeps close in to her subject at what one might call box-camera distance.]

The little red engine of the English story is bound for Dodge, Mazy, Callington, Humble, Never Over, Soke, Seven Sisters, Dumble and Home, names which I relish like those in an Edward Thomas poem, but which, foolishly perhaps, I altered in my own reading to the more familiar place names which Carol hears us say—Oamaru, Timaru, Orari, and Christchurch. Leslie Wood's pictures to *The Story of the Little Red Engine* also show a train moving through a landscape but the criticism of the point of vision which I make with the other book hardly applied here, because these landscapes seem more like the world seen from a carriage window. For Carol the coloured illustrations of woods, of sheep in fields, of country railway stations and rolling hills all recaptured her own journey north through Canterbury, while I found them pleasing for the same reasons that I like John Piper and Edward Bawden. So often my only pleasure in a picture book comes from awareness of Carol's enjoyment. Every book which satisfies her cannot satisfy me aesthetically. This one did.

Babar and His Children, a new Jean de Brunhoff picture book, dealt with another theme close to Carol's heart, for she is now very much aware of 'her little baby' at present growing in her mother. She was absorbed by the picture of elephant babies in a pram and the fact that there were three was not remarked upon, fortunately for me. She found the idea of a pram running away down hill quite exciting, but it was in reading about this incident that I found a weakness in the illustrations. On one page the pram is shown slipping downwards, but when one turns over-leaf for another picture of the descent the pram continues downward in another direction. The pictures don't flow, and Carol kept turning the pages backwards and forwards with a puzzled expression.

Arthur in the story lets the pram slip while he is watching a procession. When this word came up Carol began to talk about the procession of Kaikorai School children whom she sees on Friday mornings; the word had a real significance for her. Again when Alexander sails on the lake I realized from her comments and general interest how much more 'lake' meant than it did when we read our first Babar book. The Christchurch visit had given her a concrete experience of what a lake actually looked like.

Babar and His Children has the real adventure quality of the

Beatrix Potter stories but the story requires too much adaptation for Carol at the present time. This would not have mattered earlier but she has begun to correct me when I alter a text and I can't remember from one day to another the precise adjustment of the text which I have made. *The Story of the Little Red Engine* has the same disadvantage so both these books have been returned to the library.

30 DECEMBER 1948

This morning was a true midsummer day. Ann and Carol were soon overtired with running about and I suggested stories under the trees. Ann asked for *Peter Rabbit,* which they have been reading about once a fortnight for a long time now. My impression is that they ask different questions every time I read the book and find something new there, much as I find something new every time I pick up *Emma* or *Middlemarch.* The children's classic seems to propagate itself like a bulb, and because of this and because Beatrix Potter's English is so pleasing, I too never become bored with Peter. Yet there are other stories that the children obviously enjoy which reduce me to internal screaming point by the time I've read them ten or twelve times.

Today it was the picture of Flopsy, Mopsy, and Cottontail gathering blackberries which caught their fancy, probably because a few days ago the two of them were over in the section beyond the bush. Together with young Margaret, Carol and Ann enjoyed the illicit pleasures of picking blackcurrants meant for jam. In the story they obviously associated the blackberries with the currants.

Once or twice lately, when I have left the house to go visiting or down to the library or when Dick has left for work in the mornings, Carol has been calling admonishments.

I had been a little puzzled because her manner and material have not been a direct imitation of what I or her father would say on like occasions. It has an alien element in it, like an unidentified flavour in a dish for which one thought one knew the recipe. I've just realized that into my normal cautions she had blended Mrs Rabbit's 'You may go into the fields and down the lane but don't go into Mr McGregor's garden.' Yesterday when I left her next door while I went to town she called back after me, 'Mummy'. Then, holding her head on one side and putting on the half-smiling, half-stern face which signals that she is acting, she said, 'Don't go on the street cars, run over and get some buns, and don't go in Mr McGregor's garden.'

Again last week before breakfast, a leisurely Sunday morning being in progress, I found Carol crawling about the hall, a 'pretendy' Peter on all fours eating invisible radishes. She bounded over to a sofa (alias toolshed) and asked me to be McGregor. I had to look under the flower pots as he did in the story while from her 'watering can' there came a realistic sneeze. That Sunday this game was played on and off all day.

After 'Peter Rabbit' I read Lucy Sprague Mitchell's *Fix It Please,* a story about a small American family. Like young children in real life Polly and Jimmy tear and break things in the course of their play. The buttons come off Polly's overalls and her mother sews them on again. Jim falls over and his knee is bandaged and painted with iodine. A broken plate is put together again with glue, a wheel is replaced on a toy cart, and the chair has a new leg made for it. Mother sews an arm back on the favourite doll, and when Polly and Jimmy fall sick the doctor comes with bag and medicine to make them well again. The book ends: 'When I grow up,' says Jimmy, 'I'll be the fix-it man.' 'And I'll be the fix-it mummy,' says Polly.

Carol and Ann appreciated all this even if neither of their fathers is capable of the carpentry feats of the book parent. Carol began to chat away about the carpenter who had mended her pram and fixed her bed. Thinking about the book I remembered a theatre manager who once said to me about the films he showed, 'This is strictly an action house.' Something of the sort could be said of *Fix It Please,* which is a book of 'happenings' as Lois Lenski's *Spring Is Here* was not. In adult terms, 'action' in a crude sense spells wild horses, guns, and sudden death, but to a child 'break' is 'action' and so is 'mend'. *Fix It Please* weaves all this familiar material of a young child's life into a lively narrative free from cautionary moralizing. I found the tone of the story sane and healthy. Parents are people who patch up those things which have been accidentally broken, a fair presentation, whereas in another book Carol was given, *Bad Mousie,* the whole stress lies on the awful wickedness of an act of breaking. [See entry for 10 March 1949.]

9 JANUARY 1949

An opossum was on the roof last night. We all had a wakeful night. After breakfast, too tired for housework, I again read Carol *Fix It Please.* As we read you could see her making comparisons between her life and the lives of Polly and Jimmy in the story. 'Look, Polly's got a blue coat just like me.' 'I've got a zipper on the *back* of *my* jersey.' The bandage in the book was greeted as enthusiastically in literature as in life, though she remarked accusingly, 'You don't give me iodine.' When we came to the incident of the smashed plate mended with glue, a process Carol has never seen, she turned to me in some concern, saying, 'Have we any glue?' And once more when we read about the home carpentry she remarked, 'Mr B. mended my push-cart.'

[Throughout the next six months Carol continued to measure herself and me against this book and I recorded this very fully in my complete diary. In February I noted arguments about changing from nightgowns to pyjamas 'like Ann and Polly'. In April she was asking us to buy a car to take her to the country like Polly and Jimmy, and when winter came she wanted overalls like her heroine.]

There have been some stumbling blocks to Carol's understanding of the story. The incident of the mended doll was one. Dear-Anne, Polly's doll, is shown in one picture without an arm and in the next picture whole and in her right mind. Unfortunately in the second picture the mended doll is shown in different clothes from those she wears on her first appearance. When action in a picture book progresses like this from one page to another I do not think that a child automatically accepts the fact that it is another picture of the same thing or situation at another stage. If a character changes garments between one page and the next, a further complication is introduced. [For months afterwards when we read this book together Carol had difficulty in understanding that these two pictures represented the same doll.]

[On 9 March 1949, I noted another confusion which arose in connection with the father's carpentry. There is an illustration of the father mending a chair and in the upper corner of the same page there is a small inset picture of a father's hands with a saw cutting the piece of wood to be used in the mending process shown below. Here we were bogged.]

C: Whose are those hands?

D: Those are Daddy's hands.

C: No, *those* are Daddy's hands (pointing at full picture).

D: That's another picture of Daddy's hands, Carol.

C: Daddy hasn't got four hands. Are those Mummy's hands?

Weakly I said 'Yes', but the riposte came quickly: 'Mummy doesn't use a saw.'

This matter was never satisfactorily settled. On 24 May she was still asking about those two lots of hands.]

24 JANUARY 1949

For the last six weeks or so Carol has been coming to my bed between 6 a.m. and 6.30 a.m. demanding a story. I usually make her one, letting her choose what it shall be about. Before Christmas a story about a birthday was her favourite, but after 25 December requests for this story ceased, birthdays being outdazzled by the greater glory of Christmas. Her current favourite is Santa Claus in two versions: (a) what he brought Carol, and (b) precisely what occurred the day Carol went to see him at a department store. The latter is told in microscopic detail. I have been reproached for not mentioning locking a door on leaving home, in this artless narrative. Similarly, another story, 'going to Roslyn' must be also told without generalization or elision. 'Carol's mummy went to the fruit shop and bought a lettuce, a pound of tomatoes, and two pounds of peaches, and then she went to the fish shop and bought some sole fillets and a crayfish, and then she went to the cake shop and bought a sponge because visitors were coming to tea, and then—she went to the ice-cream shop and bought Carol an ice cream "in a pink cone".'

There is something quite fatuous about such 'stories' when written down, yet they are quite beloved narratives told over and over again nearly every morning.

Books which I have read to her recently are a library book *Surprise for Davy* by Lois Lenski, and two of the Christmas Golden Books *Toys* and *Animals of Farmer Jones*.

Surprise for Davy has been read to Carol half a dozen times, and once to a large group of the Garfield Avenue children, John, Ann, Margaret, and Carol, when they all chorused, almost in unison, 'Read it again.' To look at, the book is one of those deceptively simple texts whose value one could so easily underestimate if one hadn't read it aloud to children and seen their response. Published in New York, *Surprise for Davy* is the story of a birthday, and I realized on reading it that birthdays must be standard over the English-speaking world, with the parcels to be opened, the party, the games of ring o'roses, the cake, the candles, the ice-cream and paper hats, sing 'Happy birthday' and everyone goes home. Lois Lenski must at some time have coped with a child asking eternally, 'What are their names?' because in the pictures of guests at Davy's party every name is given. Books by parents are so much easier on other parents.

Carol has enjoyed *Animals of Farmer Jones* as much as *Surprise for Davy* but I have enjoyed it more, as the animal pictures are very well done indeed, and I am not usually moved to enthusiasm by pictures of kine and kindred. Rudolph Freund's illustrations, unlike many in the Golden Book series, really have been made by an individual artist with a style recognizably his own. The plot, or more modestly expressed the scheme of the book, is the feeding of Farmer Jones's flock of animals. 'It is supper time on the farm. The animals are very hungry. But where is Farmer Jones?' The story follows each animal to his place on the farm and each animal with his own particular grunt or gobble exclaims he is hungry and asks 'Where is Farmer Jones?' Supper time is at six o'clock. Farmer Jones looks at his watch and collects the fodder—'oats for the horse, grain for the cows, . . . bones for the dog, milk for the cat and mush for the pigs.' The story then goes back over its tracks as each animal gets his food and grunts in gratitude.

That is all—the everyday life on an ordinary American farm shaped into a narrative for a three- and four-year-old—yet it is precisely this form and shaping which is as rare in contemporary stories as it is common in the traditional nursery tales.

On the first reading of the story, the refrain 'Where is Farmer Jones?' worried Carol. She wanted to turn over the page and find him. I have noticed before that a story of this type, which to a small child involves real suspense, is often more satisfactory on its second and later readings. A surprise or climax to a child is no whit less a surprise or climax when she knows the ending; indeed when a child knows the ending she can savour the suspense without *real* concern. The first time she heard the story Carol could not be sure that Farmer Jones would ultimately be found.

[*Animals of Farmer Jones* became that year one of Carol's best loved books and Farmer Jones himself a household myth like Mother Goose. She developed a passionate interest in animal diet. 'What do tigers eat? What do fishes eat? What do birds?' Throughout 1949 we were answering such questions, and although I have not read her this story for the last six months it is still part of her background. A year after the original diary entry was made we went rowing up Brighton River, and she was delighted to have a farm-house pointed out—'That's where Farmer Jones lives.' A good children's book is like a gifted man in an obscure place. It is not easy for an observer outside the circle to estimate just how far or how deep that influence may reach. April 1950.]

13 FEBRUARY 1949

On Christmas Day Carol saw four-weeks-old David being fed, and I overheard her say to his mother with slight scorn in her voice. 'I'm getting a new baby, but not one like that

—one that can sit up.' Clearly her picture of the coming baby was one like Alan next door who is a year old now, and just as clearly she had to be warned what to expect. Two weeks ago, therefore, I borrowed from the library Marjorie Flack's *The New Pet*. This book has pictures of a new-born baby as he must appear to everyone except mother, red, cross-eyed, with foetus-like legs. I'm not surprised that Italian painters of Madonna and Child always show Mary with a glamorous child of six months. In *The New Pet* the older brother and sister see a yelling new-born baby with amazement and a suspicion of horror, justifiable emotions which vanish as the story continues and they see the child learn to smile, to crawl, to stand and finally, as a climax, to walk.

When I read this book to Carol she talks about 'my little baby' while the child in the story is young, and then when he reaches an erect position she begins to talk about Alan. It is a very useful book although the opening part of the story is open to criticism. Briefly, the children want a pet, their mother promises them one and they begin to discuss what it is likely to be—a dog? a goldfish? They do not know. Mother disappears away to hospital and comes back with a baby, the much promised new pet. As a device for preparing children for a baby I can't imagine a sillier one. What little boy hoping for a dog would be pleased with a baby? Obviously nothing about the real origins of the baby has been told to the children.

Again to revert to my ancient bugbear: 'It might be' situations are illustrated. 'It might be a goldfish'—and there in the picture *is* a goldfish.

Pretending is now in fashion with Carol and all her friends. During January she sometimes played in the mornings with Raymond, who is three, and John, who is nearly five. Many of their games, to judge from the noise, are wildly exciting, particularly a version of 'hide and seek'. 'You be the hunter and I'll be the wolf,' says Carol, who seems to 'boss' the boys in these imaginative games, in notable contrast to her play with Ann which is truly co-operative. Then suggestions come from both sides. Yesterday the two girls came to eat me up. I was Goldilocks they told me, inspired by another kindergarten story. As I listened to them I thought how useful among small children is a core of stories known to them all, for upon this they can build all manner of games and share a common heritage with one another. Likewise the nursery rhymes which adults of all ages recite to children make a common bond between the adult and younger listener. However, with a newer generation of adults even these nursery rhymes are losing their place. People occasionally talk to Carol about Micky Mouse or Donald Duck or Bambi and she doesn't know what they are talking about. She has not been given any Disney books, and it appears that she is being cut off from what has come to be a contemporary folklore.

19 FEBRUARY 1949

Dick took Ann and Carol over to see the elephants at the circus. Ann said, 'Just like the Babar book,' and Carol, 'I want to see some little elephants.'

Last night I read or rather talked to her about the pictures in *Animal Babies,* another Golden Book with an inadequate text. It seems to me that one finds much more sheer silliness in writing about animals than one ever does in writing about children. (Compare the lush sentiment of *Black Beauty* with the austerity of *High Wind in Jamaica*.) However Carol enjoyed the animal pictures and listened attentively to what I could tell her about them, which wasn't very much. This morning she spent half an hour in bed pointing, 'That's an elephant,' and 'That's a monkey.'

Another Golden Book we have read again is Edith Osswald's *Toys.* The text is precise and detailed from the child's point of view, but still to my mind banal and unlovely. In all justice I remind myself that Carol seems to like it. [But phrases from the book have never flowed over into her speech and conversation, which is a fair test of the quality of prose intended for children.] I have an impression when I read this book to her that she is not so much listening as looking at the illustrations with my voice as a background noise. One cannot support a statement like that, but with an arm round a child whom one loves one feels almost literally a varying tenseness as a child hears different stories—the rhythmical shake as one reads a nursery rhyme, the tense interest when one first read *Peter Rabbit,* the relaxed attention given to *Toby's House,* the flaccid non-listening that precedes a wriggle and a dart away when I pick up Lear. In this way I believe I know when Carol is barely hearing the words I am reading. She listens to a rhythmical chant like this where a boy is banging at a peg board,

> *Bang! Bang!*
> *Swing the hammer!*
> *Pound the peg!*
> *Bang!*
> *Down goes the big peg.*
> *Down goes the little peg.*

But most of the time she is looking at the pictures of these American children with their Aladdin store of toys. When I look at these pictures, of a toy barn packed with wooden animals, six varieties of toy horses, exquisitely made dolls' furniture, I long to ransack an American toyshop. Carol, however, wants to look at pictures of toys similar to those with which she herself has played, for with that unaffected provincialism of childhood she likes best what she knows best. As it seems years since we have had one of King John's 'big bouncing indiarubber balls' she passes quickly over illustrations of them just as she does with pictures of a jigsaw puzzle. On the other hand she examines intently the pictures of children playing with telephone, wash-tub, doll's pram, and carpentry set. She has never played with hammer and nails but she has watched and interrogated the two carpenters next door who are working on the new room for Alan. What attracts her most however is the train pictures. She had watched open-mouthed one morning last week while John's mother demonstrated the Hornby train on the verandah. His father had made stations, signals, and tunnels and the whole set-up looked like one of those classic *Punch* jokes about Christmas presents which adults cannot leave alone. Then again recently on Sunday walks, Dick, legally or illegally, has let her run about inside empty vans shunted on to sidings in the deserted railway yards. Carol knows all about overhead bridges, tracks, and signal boxes.

The train pictures in *Toys* have raised a problem which headmasters used to mention years ago when we were discussing the use of American books in New Zealand school libraries —the very different terminology of even standard American compared with English. At the time I did not take the matter very seriously, but now I do. With the book *Toys* I have to translate box-car to luggage van, tank car to petrol waggon. Gondola I did not translate because I couldn't, while caboose seemed a correct word. However Dick, hearing me read caboose was wrath indeed. 'What may I ask is wrong with good old English guard's van?' We argued, and the Oxford dictionary had the last word: 'caboose, a cooking room on ship's deck.'

5 MARCH 1949

Surprise for Davy, now referred to as 'My good birthday book', has been read two or three times a week all this year, sometimes because Carol asks for it, and sometimes, if I feel tired at the end of the day, because it is the most quickly read book she possesses. She has begun to count the children at the party, 'One, two, five, six, nine, ten.'

Last week she began asking for her 'chooky book', which I took some time to decipher as a request for *Mother Goose*. Dick often finds it difficult to know which book she wants, as every story is given a special name of her own. The Rojan-kovsky illustrated rhymes were finally found under a pile of old shoes in her wardrobe. She was really excited to have the long-lost book again and began to talk the rhymes over to herself. On several afternoons since the book was found she has sat talking contentedly with it for half an hour at a time.

5 MARCH 1949

The early morning demand for stories continues, having grown into a convention which cannot be broken. This morn-ing, as a change from *Farmer Jones* and *Fix It Please,* I read to her from Milne's *Now We Are Six,* beginning with *Busy,* the poem which starts 'I think I am a muffin man'. I hadn't realized before what a completely 'threeish' poem this is with its rapid transitions from one impersonation to another. Like the character portraits in Gesell and Ilg's *Infant and Child in the Culture of Today,* it seems to be written about *our* child. Carol is always being someone or something, and her aliases have the same fleeting duration as Christopher Robin's. When we came to the refrain of *Busy,*

> *Round about*
> *And round about*
> *And round about I go,*

I could feel her small body bounding in time with the rhythm of the poem.

Down by the Pond ('I'm fishing. Don't talk anybody, don't come near') like *Simple Simon,* is linked in her mind with the fishermen of the Sunday walks. On my second reading of the poem she began to ask about lines and where Christopher Robin put his fish. I can't remember all her questions but I could see that she was comparing what she had seen with what the boy in the poem did. She did not understand at first that the pictures of a boy newting and a boy fishing were one and the same person. Again and again, there are these indications of how slight is the small child's sense of continuity.

Other poems she liked were *Furry Bear* ('He's in a cage,' she said, 'and he can't get out.') and the *Swing Song.* Because I'm usually with her when we go down to our swing she looked curiously round the picture and said, 'Where's the mummy?' Another favourite was the *Cradle Song* that begins 'O Timothy Tim has ten pink toes'. Obviously she connected this with Timothy in *The New Pet.* She asked for it again tonight and I left her going to sleep saying 'O Timothy Tim'.

Reading *Now We Are Six,* where Christopher Robin in traditional English smock might be a little girl, I noticed something Jean first pointed out, her tendency to make every possible 'he' into a 'her'.

10 MARCH 1949

During the last four weeks, we have had four sessions with *Bad Mousie,* Donica's story, written by her mother Martha Dudley. I did not feel enthusiastic about *Bad Mousie* when it was first given to Carol and I put the book away in a drawer, where it has remained until she found it during a rummage three weeks ago. We have read it many times now, and I have seen

Bad Mousie come to equal the *Fix It* book and *Animals of Farmer Jones* in popularity, albeit a popularity of a subtly different kind from that which the other two enjoy with her. This is Carol's first crime story, and she asks for it with a wicked look in her eye. This is her Dashiel Hammett, her James Cain and Raymond Chandler, or something darker, her Raskolnikov perhaps.

Bad Mousie, who shares the home of Donica and her mother, is bad 'because no one taught him to be good'. It is a commentary on middle-class American life and manners that most of his crimes are offences against the code of the house-proud. As I read the book to Carol I remembered those spotless American houses. Dutch clean were they all, and I can guess how easy it might be for a child to commit naughtiness within them. Some of this mouse's 'wickedness' is more serious, more wantonly naughty, but it is still a wanton naughtiness provoked, I think, or at least suggested by an over-tidy, over-clean environment. To quote:

He hid one of Donica's new mittens and made mud tracks all over the rug whenever he came in, threw clean socks into the bath-tub, pulled the top off the powder-can and spilled powder all over the rug; he tangled Donica's hair and scattered her ribbons on the floor, he tipped over things and spilled cocoa and milk and orange juice, pulled books out of the bookshelves, and painted the floor with a bottle of shoe polish, emptied the buttons out of the button-box.

Donica in the story loves her Mousie but her mother does not. When the parent is particularly irritated by the mouse she sends him packing, takes her broom, sweeps him from the house and locks the door. There the mouse waits till dark when he creeps back through a hole in the wall. Next day he again misbehaves and on this occasion the mother says,

'I'm going to put you in a box and close it tight and throw it in my wash-tub full of water.' This she does, but the box comes apart and the mouse is reprieved. Again he misbehaves and the mother threatens to feed him to the night-owl. 'So she took him and tied him with three white strings to the fence in the back-yard. Then she put a yellow ribbon around his neck so that the owl could see him better in the dark and fly down and gobble him up.'

Again the mouse escapes, again returns home, and again misbehaves. To quote again:

When Mummy came home and found the terrible mess he had made, she grabbed him by his little string tail and she pressed her lips together hard and thought of a way to get rid of him. At last she decided to let the wind blow him away. She got out her oldest umbrella and fastened Mousie to the handle with an old belt. Then she carried him up on to the roof and opened the umbrella so the wind could blow him off right up into the sky.

The mouse rests on a cloud, safe there until the cloud drips away into rain and he is dropped into the sea. By now repentance is setting in and when the mouse swims ashore and returns to Donica's house 'he wiped his muddy little feet on the doormat so Mummie's rugs would stay clean'. Donica is asked if she will teach the mouse to be good. 'She showed him what not to touch, . . . to wipe up milk, . . . to pick up books, . . . to set the table, . . . wipe the forks and spoons.' Mother is overjoyed and the story closes with all three—mother, Mousie, and Donica—dancing in a ring. Virtue has been successfully inculcated and a mouse is housebroken.

I have found it difficult to systematize my thoughts and feelings about this book into any settled opinion of its merits and demerits. Most disturbing is the element of sadism in the

book. When I first read *Bad Mousie* to Carol I softened the
account of the mouse's ordeal and did not read the whole
detailed purgatory until I overheard Dick read the book as it
was written. I need not have worried, for Carol was not unduly
harrowed or disturbed, although the book did represent something entirely new to her in story telling.

The mouse is obviously an *alter ego* or imaginary playmate
of the child Donica, a scapegoat, the narrative of whose crimes
is intended as an 'awful warning'. So too, in an ancient time
did the adviser at a court warn his monarch of specific errors
in the form of a fable. By discussing the misdemeanour as
though it is committed by someone other than a king or one's
child, the story-teller-cum-adviser removes the crime from its
personal association. It is seen as 'a deed' not as 'your deed',
and the wrong-doer is able to make a moral judgment on that
action without specifically accusing himself or being accused.
[In the French film *The Baker's Wife* there is an instance of this
kind towards the close of the film when the baker addresses
his complaint to a wandering cat, not to his erring wife.]

But to return to earth, Carol at the moment shows an almost
passionate willingness to lay tables.

14 MARCH 1949

On Friday evening she began to demand her animal book.
She didn't want *Animals of Farmer Jones* but *Animal Babies,*
which she had been read a couple of times in February. She
was delighted to have the book again. 'I haven't had this for
a long time.' She seems to be acquiring a sense of distance
backward in time, which is something rather different from
the mere referring to things which happened in the past, for
now she is aware of a *varying* space between the now and the
then. She notices which dress she has not been wearing or

food which has been out of season and has returned to the
table. 'We haven't had pears for a long time.'

On Friday's reading of *Animal Babies* she liked the camel
and his mother particularly. If she can't find a mummy and
daddy in this book she is clearly disappointed. I must find one
for her or explain where the missing one might be. She has
developed a keen family sense, stimulated probably by her
knowledge of the coming baby who should be here today.
'We're a family,' says Carol. 'I'm a family. You're a family.
You're a family. We're a family.'

When we came to the kangaroo in the story I brought over
the felt one which her grandmother had made for her and
she looked at the toy with more than usual interest, for this,
by one of those unpredictable aversions of childhood, has never
been a favoured animal. She noticed that the baby kangaroo
had fallen from the mother's pouch, and went to find it. That
evening she took the kangaroo to bed with her and for the
first time showed it some real affection. I was reminded of a
weakness of my own in adolescence, and perhaps much later,
when an emotion or an experience would appear so much
more 'valuable' if one chanced to encounter it in print.

Any picture at all interests her now. Dick has given me
one of Black's Colour Books on Russia published about 1910.
I tried to read this the other afternoon as Carol seemed settled
at some play, but from the other side of the room she saw
I had a book with pictures and came over with demands for
'talk about them'. She wanted only the coloured pictures not
the photogravure. 'Those aren't the pretty ones.' I enjoyed
the sheer humour of this session while Carol made a picture
of imperial Russia after her own image. The Kremlin became
a town, the Neva a harbour, the droshky drivers so many
daddies in big overcoats.

In all this, a child's first experiences with stories and pictures, there is an immense amount of explaining to do. In sheer quantity of words, the actual stories Carol has read to her represent only a fraction beside all my amplifying remarks at the time of reading and afterwards. Sometimes when Dick is answering

Carol's questions I see that because so much which happens to her is out of his sight and so many of her references are riddles to him, he cannot, try as he will, see what point her question is trying to reach. Yet an understanding father must know more of a child's background than any teacher. I am baffled to know how infant school teachers manage at the beginning when their knowledge of a child's particular meanings and emphases to words must be so slight.

22 MARCH 1949

Carol has spent several days in bed, and although up is still home from kindergarten and separated from playmates. As I do not leave the house, we have developed one of those close-knit lives of the pre-kindergarten days when I almost knew what she was thinking about. It has been an intensive reading period, but I am now too sleepy after dinner to make adequate notes on it all. Late pregnancy is like Marvell's vegetable love, 'vaster than empires and more slow'.

When Dr B. came the first time Carol obviously remembered her *Fix It* book, for she had seen no doctor within her memory. Her eye fell on the stethoscope. 'I don't want to be fixed.' When she got up she broke one of her china doll's plates and insisted that I should mend it 'like the book'. Before this she has seen pieces thrown into the rubbish bin without a qualm. I had no glue so I used seccotine applied with my fingers instead of a brush, which she observed and commented upon with disapproval. However, once the plate was mended her delight was obvious. 'Look what my mummy did—just like Polly's mummy.'

On Thursday it rained hard during breakfast and she began to say, 'Drip, drip, drip'. I remembered the incident in *Bad Mousie* where the outlawed mouse sits on a cloud until drip, drip, drip, it begins to dissolve into rain. She has begun to tell me long elaborate stories. This morning's narrative was typical: its heroine as usual someone called 'my girl'. 'My girl' had a long record of delinquency, all the crimes of the bad mouse's calendar combined with Carol's misdemeanours of the last thirty-six hours or so. I am rather weary now, and poor Carol easily offends. Her fusion of the two crime sheets in her story was interesting, as a piece of adult writing can be when it is done by a friend with whose life and mind one is familiar. One can discern the original experiences which have been transmuted into a new work of art. In her story of 'my girl' Carol was making a new tale for the chimney corner, disinterested story-making perhaps, but she was also projecting her particular offences on to a neutral screen.

[The diary breaks off here abruptly. Victoria was born four days later, and in the general change in all our lives no further entries were made until the middle of May. And no reading was done. Life temporarily banished literature altogether.]

4

Three and a Half to Four

I see that I have written nothing in this diary since four days before Victoria was born, and as far as I remember I have read nothing very much to Carol since them. There are barely enough hours in the day in which to feed a baby five times and the others three, much less time for luxuries like reading. Carol has been ill off and on with bronchitis which seems to promise a dismal winter. Luckily Barbara has given her a vast store of paper dolls and has called in several times and read to her, for which two of us are grateful. The other afternoon while I fed Victoria in comparative peace, Carol said she would read to Barbara out of *Animal Babies*. Barbara told me afterwards that she was able to say the names of nearly all the animals in the book, squirrel, donkey, kangaroo, whale and tiger etc. Only chipmunk, raccoon and hippopotamus defeated her. Carol at present has a passionate interest in animals, an almost entirely 'literary' interest really because real animals figure rarely on her landscape. Fortunately Dr B. has a loving interest in natural history, and he early established good relations with her by talking about birds and worms and insects, the sort of conversations Dick and I never have with the child. It is not until I hear some other adult with Carol —Beth singing 'Cherry Ripe', or Christopher chatting about how a box is made, or Dr B. on the life-cycle of the common or garden worm—that I realize how much Dick and I omit to mention when we are talking to her. As parents we try to give her as complete a picture of the world as we can, but unwittingly we leave out so much. As Christopher said on Christmas Day, perhaps with justice, 'Your education of Carol is purely social—it's all about people and never about things.'

While ill, Carol has been sleeping for a long time during the afternoon, and as a result she is often awake till eight or nine in the evening. Dick has read to her each evening from *Millions of Cats, Little White Gate,* some of the Golden Books, and *Mike Mulligan and His Steam Shovel* by Virginia Lee Burton. I gave her this after we had had a bulldozer literally on our front door-step. Part of the 'Redwood' estate has been sold as a building section which was levelled in an awesome mechanical way last week. I carried Carol downstairs in dressing-gown and blanket to see the bulldozer but she was frightened by the noise and the chaos of mud.

About my only reading to Carol over the last six weeks has been from *When We Were Very Young,* although reading is barely the term to use. While I nurse Victoria, Carol often brings up the Milne book, and if I keep my eyes on her and recite hard, I manage to avoid any tantrums during the feeding. 'Quietness is most essential,' says my Plunket book. 'The mother and baby should be in a quiet room where they will not be disturbed at feeding time and the mother should give her whole attention to the child while he is at the breast . . . the mere fact of talking or reading a book may alter the flow

of the mother's milk, distract the baby and make him dissatisfied with his meal.' Make *him* dissatisfied, yes; but not our
Victoria. I have to talk to Carol all the time or she will make
a disturbance. I recite *John has great big waterproof boots on* or
James, James, Morrison, Morrison, and carry on long discussions
about Buckingham Palace, the duties of soldiers on guard, and
the precise whereabouts of the King. Child at the breast or
not, I converse about elephants, the circus, bison, and the feeding habits of butterflies.

There seems to be a tremendous mental growth round about
this time. Am very tired and wish I could write this up more
fully.

23 MAY 1949

Carol has found *The Tale of Mrs Tiggy-Winkle* again, and
I read it to her this afternoon when for once unaccountably
there was a breathing-space in life. It seems weeks since we
settled down for an old-fashioned 'pre-baby' spell of reading
together, and she was tremendously excited as, face glowing,
she gave the usual 'cuddle up for stories'. When I read Mrs T.
to her before, I omitted to make a note in the diary, but I
seem to remember finding the story in some respects unsatisfactory. Today however I thought the story had some of the
real charm of living about it, the 'poetry of Monday morning',
and these feelings Carol obviously shared, although there were
still some passages she did not understand.

Mrs Tiggy-Winkle is probably the only English classic with
a washerwoman as heroine, although as Margaret Lane[*] has
commented, Mrs T. 'is far more than a washerwoman; she is
an accomplished laundress. In her "nice clean kitchen with a
flagged floor and wooden beams—just like any other farm

[*]Margaret Lane. *The Tale of Beatrix Potter* (Warne, 1946), p. 124.

kitchen" there is a "nice hot singey smell" and Mrs Tiggy-Winkle expertly ironing and goffering and shaking out frills. "Oh yes if you please'm, I'm an excellent clear-starcher!" '

Lucie, the child in this story, loses her pocket handkerchief and in search of it she goes off over a stile, up a hill path, by a spring and through Mrs Tiggy-Winkle's door. This afternoon as we looked for a moment at the pictures before I began to read, Carol wanted to call Lucie 'Goldilocks'. However, once the story was begun she accepted the name Lucie, and listened intently but without comment until Lucie was half-way up the hillside and her home lay 'right down away below'. 'Who is with her? Why is she by herself?' I realized with a pang that Carol has never gone anywhere by herself.

The next picture showed a spring bubbling out from a hillside, and the one after it showed Lucie outside Mrs Tiggy-Winkle's door. This transition came too fast for Carol. 'Is Lucie in the water?' I had some difficulty in convincing her that Lucie had walked on past the stream. When we came to Mrs T. discussing her capacities as a starcher, Carol was delighted. She had watched me make starch a few mornings before and had been allowed to dip a tray-cloth in the basin. My memories, too, were stirred, and I could hear my mother talking to me as a child about goffering irons she had once owned. All the detail of the care of clothes, washing, starching, ironing, and airing fascinated Carol, but the close of the story where Mrs Tiggy-Winkle dematerializes was rather unsatisfactory.

How small she had grown—and how brown and covered with prickles. Why, Mrs Tiggy-Winkle was nothing but a hedgehog. . . . Now some people say that little Lucie had been asleep upon the stile—but then how could she have found three clean pocket handkerchiefs and a penny with a silver safety pin?

'Where are Mrs Tiggy-Winkle's clothes?' said Carol, and

turned to the end-papers in an effort to find them. I couldn't really satisfy her about this ending or non-ending. She isn't ready to be left in the air with a riddle.

When we had finished with Mrs Tiggy-Winkle, she asked me for *The Little White Gate,* Aileen Findlay's story of a suburban gate and the people who use it, family, milkman, paper-man, and coal-man. All this fits in very well with our daily 'island life' in Garfield Avenue, more particularly since the gate next door was broken recently, and Carol watched the mending and repainting with keen interest. She was thrilled as I read about the broken gate in the story. When she gave me the book to read, however, the first thing she said was, 'This book has a hedgehog in it too.' So it had, in one sentence. She waited expectantly while I read, 'All night long it stood in the darkness. It saw the moon come up and it watched the dark shadows the trees made in the garden. Sometimes a hedgehog came by and sometimes a field-mouse.' The passage is repeated at the end of the story when another day is over. At this time of year more than in the summer such a passage has a richer meaning for a child. Carol sees our moon come up, the shadows in our garden, and the darkness outside.

After the reading was over I fed the baby while Carol spent the time 'ironing', a perfect Mrs Tiggy-Winkle. She turned the word Tiggy-Winkle over on her tongue, with the usual pleasure she gets from polysyllables, 'animals', 'hospital', or 'exciting'. And as she ironed she repeated to herself quietly, 'Sometimes a hedgehog came by and sometimes a mouse.' Then 'mouse' reminded her of *Bad Mousie,* and she wandered off in chat about the Night Owl.

24 MAY 1949

When I told Carol we could have stories she brought *Fix*

It Please, which she still calls 'the Polly book'. In the part of
the story where the slide fastener is broken she played 'pretendy'
zip fasteners against my dress. There was no direct identification with Polly and Jimmy being sick, but she was vastly
interested in their medicine. 'Does it have a nasty taste?' she
asked, for her doctor had given her two, a sweet and a bitter.

Tonight in the bathroom she turned, sudden in accusation.
'I used to have a sleepy book. We'll get it from the library.'

10 JUNE 1949

A week ago when I was too tired to make a record Carol
took out *Bad Mousie* and 'read' it to herself while I fed Vicky.
For twenty minutes she talked about the book, which seems
to have a special significance to her these days when I resemble
a beast of uncertain temper.

This afternoon Ann and Alan came in to play. I offered to
read them all *Millions of Cats* but Carol brought over a new
Beatrix Potter, *The Tale of Mrs Tittlemouse.* Alan, who is
eighteen months old now, insisted on climbing up beside me.
'Book, book,' quoth he and sat eyes wide, without a wriggle
or murmur as I talked. Ann listened happily too, but half-
way through Carol climbed down from the sofa and went
over to her blocks which she began to bang noisily.

I began to read *Millions of Cats* to the other two, and Carol
returned. We have had this two of three times in the last
three months now and it is always a favourite, particularly the
lines 'hundreds and thousands and millions and billions and
trillions of cats'. Three pairs of eyes shone, and I had a sudden
picture in my mind's eye of those Pittsburgh children to whom
I told folk-tales in a library story-hour twelve years ago. One
learns in situations like these the literal meaning of the word
spell-bound.

22 JUNE 1949

I had promised Carol a visit to the library, so this morning I took her with Ann and the baby down to the children's department. They rushed towards the racks of picture books full of exclamations. 'Ann's got that book.' 'Look at Snippy and Snappy!'

When we got home I asked Judith, the new child in the flat below, to join us for some stories. As on the occasion two weeks ago when our reading was shared with other children, Carol was neither happy nor attentive. We began with *Tom Kitten*. Carol barely listened, but Judith's eyes were sparkling as she repeated 'Naughty, naughty, naughty' at the kitten's misdemeanours. Ann said not one word except to chime in, 'Pit, pat, waddle, pat', as the ducks go off down the hard high-road.

Ann and Carol next asked for *Snippy and Snappy*, which they heard at kindergarten some months ago. Again, as I read, Carol would not listen, but repeated 'Snip, snap, snip, snap' in a way that I knew was meant to be annoying. During the last few months her behaviour has been difficult in a whole variety of ways, much as one expects when a second child enters the picture, but I had never foreseen that she would behave badly during stories—certainly it is only when other children are present that she refuses to listen. When *Snippy and Snappy* was finished I intended to give up the stories, as Carol was obviously in no mood for them. However, she pleaded for *The Good-night Moon,* one of the library books we borrowed this morning, so I continued. This time she listened happily and asked for the book again in bed tonight.

The Good-night Moon is a truly original book written by Margaret Wise Brown, author of our 'sleepy book', and illustrated by Clement Hurd, whose first work of all in children's

book illustration was for the American edition of Gertrude
Stein's *World Is Round*. And Gertrude Stein I think would
have approved this book, *The Good-night Moon*. In eight
double-page coloured pictures with interleaved black and
whites, the story tells of a nursery room darkening as the
day fades; the colours, at first brilliant and saturated, emerald
walls, emerald and yellow curtains, red carpet, red bed, and
a red doll's house, all dim and fade dramatically as night comes
on and the good-night moon shines in the sky. I remember a
short story I read once about a blind man who recovers his
sight and watches the light disappear at sundown on that first
day. This picture book to me was a similar adventure, an
aesthetic pleasure heightened of course by personal joy in
finding Carol still and happy after all the alarums and excursions of the day. 'Just the two of us,' she said as I began to read,

> *In the great green room*
> *There was a telephone*
> *And a red balloon*
> *And a picture of . . .*

At this point one should turn the page but Carol was not
ready. 'You haven't said about the rabbit on the bed.' She
held the page down and went round the room pointing out
all the things I hadn't said. When I was finally allowed to turn
the page, she saw overleaf two black and white enlargements
of the two pictures in the room, 'The cow jumping over the
moon', and 'Three bears'. Confused by the break from coloured
to halftone, she turned back to make sure that these were the
pictures from the wall.

Over the page to tuppence coloured the text continues:

> *And two little kittens*
> *And a pair of mittens,*
> *And a little toy house*
> *And a young mouse.*

Carol: That isn't a toy house. That's a doll's house. Who lives there?

D: The dolls.

C: Do they have a fire?

D: Yes.

C: Do the dolls make it?

D: Yes.

C: No they don't. Dolls can't make fires.

D: Just pretendy.

C: Where's the mouse going?

D: Across the room.

I see her trace a route for the mouse round the clothes horse and behind the rocking chair over to the doll's house. This mouse moves across the pages as the story progresses and as we turned each page one of her first actions was to look for him. At the end of the book where the page is darkness itself dimly coloured this was quite a feat. [In the following month, when she was sick again and read this book to herself, she would turn the pages for hours watching the mouse's progress from one side of the great green room to the other.]

Where the text reads:

> *Good night light*
> *And the red balloon*
> *Good night bears*
> *Good night chairs,*

Carol interrupted, 'You don't say good night chairs'.

> *Good night kittens,*
> *Good night mittens.*

'You don't say good night mittens.' As I read on about saying good night to all the inanimate objects of the room, Carol began to consider this a very good joke indeed, the smiles grew into shrieks of laughter. She is probably too old to appreciate this in the spirit in which it was written. Now when she makes her own distinctions between real and 'pretendy', between big girls and little girls, between mummy and woman, she makes a clear distinction between the animate and the inanimate. A doll or a toy of course comes in the animate class.

The text is inferior to the illustrations, a fact I am more aware of when I write the words down in cold blood. I noticed this hardly at all as I read to Carol; yet the words to the book are the barest commentary, the pictures are all. I am not sure of the value of rhyming texts when one has to turn a page to complete a verse or couplet, for as a child's eye roams the page in search of every detail the pause between the individual lines is a long one—if pause be the name for the interval when my voice ceases and Carol begins her voluble chatter and comment. She has very very much more to say about the book than the author has.

25 JUNE 1949

Carol ill in bed with a bronchial cold. I have read *Peter Rabbit* and *Tom Kitten* each day to her. They are her favourites among the Potter books, although I often see her looking at Mrs Tiggy-Winkle and repeating the story to herself. She has spent much of the day looking at books with intervals of cutting out paper dolls. I thought she hadn't listened to *Mrs Tittlemouse* the other afternoon when I read to Ann, Judith, and Alan, but she must have taken in more than I imagined, for she has been asking about honey drinks and saying 'Tiddly, widdly, widdly' like Mr Jackson, the toad who disturbs the order in the home of house-proud Mrs Tittlemouse. The honey drinks have only the briefest mention in the story.

When it was all beautifully neat and clean, she gave a party to five other little mice, without Mr Jackson. He smelt the party and came up the bank, but he could not squeeze in at the door. So they handed him out acorn-cupsful of honey-dew through the window and he was not at all offended. He sat outside in the sun and said 'Tiddly, widdly, widdly. Your very good health, Mrs Tittlemouse.'

The mouse in *The Good-night Moon* is daily followed by Carol over his course round the great green room.

3 JULY 1949

Carol returned to kindergarten on Friday morning for her third brief appearance this term. In the afternoon she went to play with Leonie and it was difficult to extricate her from this society after the solitary life she has led while sick. As a solace Leonie's mother lent her Lois Lenski's *The Little Family* which Leonie had borrowed from the library. Leonie, who has attained the dizzy heights of literacy, had been reading the book to Carol during the afternoon. Carol, overjoyed to have the book again, has dropped *Tom Kitten* and *Peter Rabbit*, those constant companions of the past weeks, and is absorbed in *The Little Family*. After listening to Leonie read the book on Friday afternoon she asked for it again in bed that night. We had it twice yesterday and once today. Every detail about the Little family must be investigated. 'What's in that door? What's in *that* door? What's in that window? Where's the dressing-table?' She still expects a picture to be all-embracing, and the bedroom picture falls short. She has also commented on the dust-caps worn by Sally Little and her mother when they clean house. 'Why don't you wear dust-caps?' The cake-making, with yellow mixture bowl and spoon-licking routines provokes comment too. I am no baker and Carol obviously feels she has missed something. Yesterday she begged me to cook, and as a sort of penance for my general crossness lately I made her chocolate balls. The minute I finished she asked to lick the spoon. Life in another respect had caught up on literature.

After the cooking I read twice from *In the Forest* by Marie Ets, the story of a small boy's dream adventure told in the first person. There are echoes in it of a child's own story telling.

> *I had a new horn and a paper hat*
> *And I went for a walk in the forest.*
> *A big wild lion was taking a nap*
> *But he woke up when he heard my horn.*
> *'Where are you going?' he said to me.*
> *'May I go too if I comb my hair?'*
> *So he combed his hair and he came too*
> *When we went for a walk in the forest.*

The story continues with the little boy meeting bears, elephants, monkeys, and kangaroos who on the cumulative pattern of the oldest nursery tales all join in a grand procession walking through the forest. Then the animals have a picnic and play traditional games, the last of which is a game of hide and seek. Among the forest trees which make a background for the whole story, the animals disperse and disappear from sight. Just when the boy is about to look for them, his father comes looking for him. 'It's late and we must go home. Perhaps they'll wait till another day.' At first I thought this ending was something of an anticlimax although Carol obviously did not think so. Later I realized that the entry of the father represented a 'smashing finish'—the animals could be dropped as the game of blocks or dolls' tea-party is dropped in real life when Carol hears Dick's footsteps on the stairs.

On the second reading yesterday at the beginning of the story Carol began to rub at the pictures of the forest trees. 'What's through there?' 'More trees,' said I. 'No, *Daddy's* through there.' In the later pages the father is shown coming through the trees, small as in the distance, and then life-size. I noticed too her quick identification of this story-book father as Daddy—perhaps the moustache did it. Fiction fathers are too often clean shaven.

In the Forest, like *The Good-night Moon*, is a little work of art, imagined not contrived. There was probably in both books an immense amount of hard work, as much as in any put-together-and-made-to-order book, but the work I feel sure followed on some preliminary flash of imagination. These are books which have been thought out but not thought up. There is a difference. *In the Forest* has what the Potter books have—shape and unity. The background of forest trees is a holding sheath to the tale like the Westmoreland landscapes in the Peter Rabbit series.

Tonight after tea I overheard Carol telling a story to the Bermot doll (so called because it was given to her by Bernard B.) about the brief Sunday walk today. 'There's a hospital. Sometimes a motor car came by and sometimes a truck. Sometimes a tram car came by and sometimes the people.' She was following the phrasing and my exact intonation of voice when I had read the passage from *The Little White Gate*, 'sometimes a hedgehog came by and sometimes a mouse'.

5 JULY 1949

At breakfast Carol began to tell us a story of which I remember this fragment only. 'Listen. It's about James James and he went marching in the forest. And in the forest do you know who he met? Mr Mr Mr Jones and Mr Jones he was very very fat.' She had drawn on at least four sources, A. A. Milne, *Animals of Farmer Jones*, *In the Forest*, and Beatrix Potter. I think Miss Potter provided the fat, as the only rotund character I recollect is Mr Jackson, the toad who invaded the tidy house of Mrs Tittlemouse.

More Potter yesterday afternoon. I read *The Tale of Benjamin Bunny,* a sequel to *Peter Rabbit,* in which Peter and Benjamin retrieve the clothes lost in McGregor's garden. With us the story opened badly for a variety of reasons. First, the picture of Mr McGregor's gig disappearing down the road to leave the scene clear for 'goings-on' was much too small for Carol's satisfaction. She could not decipher what was what or who was who. Further, the text reads, 'Little Benjamin Bunny did not want very much to see his aunt.' 'Why?' said Carol, to whom aunts are always desirable. Then Benjamin nearly tumbles upon the top of his cousin Peter, an effective incident but for this, that Peter is illustrated by ears alone. Carol pushed the picture to find more rabbit. However, once we were into the familiar ground of McGregor's garden the story went well and Carol found all kinds of unexpected trifles to please her, simple incidents related in some way to her own daily life at home.

The bulldozer which levelled the section next door took its toll of our drive, which is now rutted and harrowed. There is mud everywhere, and when I read about Benjamin and Peter walking over a bed of lettuces, 'newly raked and quite soft', how 'they left a great many odd little footmarks all over the bed' Carol smiled knowingly and examined the picture intently. There are a great many odd little footmarks all over our porch. Then there was the matter of onions. Carol who has seen me weep when preparing a stew fully realized the misery of the situation in which the two rabbits found themselves under the basket. 'It was quite dark . . . and the smell of onions was fearful; it made Peter Rabbit and little Benjamin cry.' 'Like my mummy.' A mention of shrinking too brought echoes of our domesticity. There are no long

D

stockings in the shops small enough to fit Carol who last week stood beside me in the bathroom while I tried to shrink size sixes. The fate of Peter's clothes when Mr McGregor hung them on his scarecrow needed no explanation.

Little Benjamin said the first thing to be done was to get back Peter's clothes, in order that they might be able to use the pocket handkerchief. They took them off the scare-crow. There had been rain during the night; there was water in the shoes, and the coat was somewhat shrunk. Benjamin tried on the tam o'shanter but it was too big for him.

Here I had a shock. 'What's a tam o'shanter?' said Carol, born and bred in Scottish Dunedin. 'It's a big beret,' I explained, melancholy that a good Scots word has gone from the New Zealand vocabulary.

As I read the story I found the pictures of Mr McGregor's garden gave me pleasure beyond the appeal of Beatrix Potter's pictures. Behind Mr McGregor's garden I seemed to have a picture of another garden, appearing like the real world to those E. Nesbit children who sailed through the sky on a worn-out magic carpet. (Thin threads, hence thin magic.) I began to remember a particular garden I had known as a child before I was five, one with rain barrels and grass paths between currant bushes and perennial borders.

[John Lehmann has commented on Edward Thomas that in him he 'found a fellow human being who had the same feeling as I had about the part of the garden beyond the lawn and the flower-border, and could, moreover, make exquisite poetry of it.'* Beatrix Potter is another such.]

6 JULY 1949

Latterly, Carol has come to like two or three different

*Penguin New Writing, No. 36, p. 109.

stories at one sitting in preference to a repetition of one favourite tale. However, she did give her old cry, 'Do it again', the other day when I read *Paul Alone in the World*, by Jens Sigsgaard.

Paul Alone in the World is the story of a small boy who wakes one morning to find himself the sole inhabitant of his town. There are no parents in their room—he can go where he likes; no shopkeepers behind their counter—he can take all he wants; no drivers in the trams—he may stand at the wheel. All this to an older child might well represent a delirium of joy and liberty, but to Carol, whose pleasure is the presence of people not their absence, it was stark tragedy. 'He's all by himself,' she said, overcome and deeply mournful. Paul's isolation obviously wounded and shocked her, but I had the feeling that in creating this dismay, the book provided her with the most tremendous emotional experience she has known in all her reading. However, here's the rub, this emotional experience was of a kind totally different from anything the author had planned to provide, for planned he had.

The *Horn Book Magazine* last year printed a letter from Sigsgaard to his American publisher explaining how the book came to be written.* He said that he had asked 1070 children between the ages of three and eight what they would do if they could be invisible. In most cases they had expressed a-social inclinations, and from the answers he had created a story to show how lonely the self-sufficient individual could be. To enhance the realistic effect of the story, Sigsgaard made it take the form of a dream. The story ends thus: 'Paul gave a mighty yell—and woke up. He lay in his own little bed. it was all a dream.' . . . "Oh Mummy, I dreamed I was all alone in the world and I could do anything I wanted to.

*Horn Book Magazine. January 1948, pp. 6-7.

But then I got tired of being all alone—I am glad it was just something I dreamed!"' Carol could not understand about this dream situation at all—it was as unsatisfactory as the close of Mrs Tiggy-Winkle. She turned back to the beginning of the book where Paul finds the parents' room empty and began to tell me how the mother and father were really there under the bedclothes, hidden. She told me this several times as though she were convincing herself although she made no effort to explain the absence of shopkeepers and tram-drivers. I have noticed on odd occasions before that where something occurs in a story which is quite contrary to her own observation and experiences she rejects the item or attempts to disprove it. This time she convinced herself that Paul's parents had never been absent. Similarly over another quite trivial incident she put her own interpretation on the matter. Paul is shown washing himself in a bedroom basin. 'That's not the bedroom—that's the bathroom,' said Carol. She refused to have it otherwise. No one in her experience has ever washed in a bedroom.

In this trifling incident, and in the larger question of Carol's whole response to the story, I can see the capital difficulty Sigsgaard was up against in planning a book along the lines he did. One may plan a particular book; one cannot plan what children will take from it.

There is another criticism which might be made of Sigsgaard's spur and purpose in writing a book to meet a psychological need, as the phrase goes. Adults observing children use a kind of mirror vision. As I am aware of Carol's interest in books but am half blind to her response to the world of natural history, others among my friends are affected with the same myopia. M., who is musical, says of his daughter, 'She has a keen sense of rhythm. Why even at the age of eighteen months she . . .' P. who specializes in physical education says, 'The boy has remarkably good muscular development for his age.' C., who is a school master comments, 'He isn't four yet but he can write his name.' Parents seem naturally to observe their children's abilities in terms of their own. A psychologist like Sigsgaard could be expected to take a broader view of such things, yet I wonder how much more detached than my friends he is. Sigsgaard lived in a highly disciplined society at the time he was working and writing, and during that period he observed children's secret desire for anarchy and the removal of authority. The question arises, whose wishes is Sigsgaard really observing—his own or the children's?

13 JULY 1949

Since I last wrote in this diary a week ago we have read a great deal together from the established favourites, *Tom Kitten, Mrs Tiggy-Winkle, The Good-night Moon,* and *Peter Rabbit.* I also revived *Flopsy Bunnies,* but this time it was not a success. The opening did not seem sharp enough or fast enough. Last summer when we read the book I noted that she listened 'baffled but not bored'. The other day however she was baffled and bored, both.

Of new books, her main interest has been in Lois Lenski's *Little Train,* one of the series of books about Mr Small whose role on this occasion is Engineer Small. How well Lois Lenski makes these books! She describes clearly and precisely all those processes necessary before a train is ready for a journey, water into tanks, coal into chute, the linking of carriages, the oiling and polishing—it has all the fascination of a documentary film. Happily for me, the author-illustrator labels her engine-picture carefully—headlight, steam-dome, etc. Illiterate on the subject of trains, I can put up a brave front and point authoritatively: 'That's a . . .' and 'That's a . . .'

After we returned from the holiday Carol played trains regularly, sometimes with Ann, sometimes alone with the dolls. Chairs, coal-scuttle, doll's bed and pram, cushions, rugs, everything she can lay her hands on is commandeered and made into a train, which stretches the whole length of the living-room. During the last week I have been interested to

see that this train game has been transformed with the addition of new elements from the Lois Lenski book. Previously her game has consisted chiefly in putting luggage aboard, in talking to Dr B., a fellow passenger on the Christchurch journey, saying goodbye to her father at Dunedin and greeting her grandmother in Christchurch. Now these features have disappeared and the new train game is played almost entirely from the point of view of the employees. Passengers' interests are forgotten as Carol oils wheels, shovels coal, reads her orders, pulls a whistle-cord and makes off from the sofa station for the tunnel under the table.

4-6 SEPTEMBER 1949

These last six weeks have been too eventful for anyone's comfort. I have had no chance to write a word although I see from my rough notes on the desk calendar that we have done a great deal of reading in spite of the upsets. Carol with acute bronchitis has been in and out of bed, and there were times when I longed to take to mine. Luckily Victoria, now weaned, continues in the sanguine way of all second children. We have bought a house and move in a fortnight's time. This flat is now a chaos of boxes and furled carpets.

I have read *Mrs Tiggy-Winkle* twice since I last wrote: that expert laundress continues to loom large on Carol's horizon. She often in play repeats Lucie's query: 'Have you seen my pocket handkerchief ?' and balances the habits of Mrs T. against mine: 'Why does Mrs Tiggy-Winkle hide her key under the door when she goes out? *You* don't.' When I was ironing the other day she confided that her iron was different from mine. Mrs T.'s irons were heated on the stove, a much more romantic method than mere electricity.

Bad Mousie has not been read for some three months, but Carol is still talking about it. It is not the mouse but the Night Owl of which I hear most. She has made two or three drawings of him from memory.

Toys, in the Golden Books series, was revived last week. Since we last read this Carol's experience has broadened and pictures which she once ignored, like those of finger-painting and the jig-saw puzzle, now arouse her interest. The train picture remains a favourite, as I remember it did before; but now, educated by Lois Lenski, Carol is able to point out the component parts. She sees a train as a complex whole not as one thing. Thinking over her reaction to this book I remember how at seventeen I read *Middlemarch* and thought Dorothea at twenty-odd very mature and sophisticated. Later, on the other side of Dorothea, I returned to the book and found the pages told an entirely new story. The same thing occurs with a child's book like *Toys,* and it occurred too with *Let's Play House,* which Ann has borrowed from the library and lent to Carol.

This familiar book took on new meanings because since Carol last saw it she had been attended by the doctor, has seen her own baby sister fed with a bottle, and has watched the spring-cleaning before we move house. To Carol, hearing *Toys* and *Let's Play House* over the century months of childhood, the books change their shape and significance; so too Marcel's experience is chameleon in the long, elaborate sequences of *Remembrance of Things Past.*

So much for the old pastures. The new books read are: *The Sleepy Little Lion, The Baby's Opera, Sung Under the Silver Umbrella,* and *The Story of the Little Ant,* retold from the Spanish by Nancy Freeman. Jean had given her this when she was only a year old.

The little ant's story begins when she finds a sixpence, which she wisely invests in ribbons to make herself pretty. 'Then she went home and put on her best dress and mantilla, and tied some of the ribbon round her waist, and some round her neck, and some round her wrists and some round her ankles.' This done she goes out into the world to find a husband, that feminine equivalent of seeking one's fortune. The test of suitability which she applies is a purely conversational one. After talking to a dog, a bull, a bear, and a rooster, she decides that all their voices are too loud for comfortable living, and she settles finally upon Pedro, a mouse with an innocuous squeak. After their wedding these two live happily together for some time—then disaster. While the ant is out at the market the mouse husband falls into the soup cauldron. The ant is still weeping for the drowned Pedro when she hears a tiny squeak.

There was Pedro. He had managed to climb out of the cauldron. He was very wet, very frightened and dripping with soup. Yellow lentil soup was streaming from his whiskers and his paws and down his tail on to the floor. There was a dreadful mess. The little ant quickly rubbed him dry with hot towels and put him to bed. When he was warm and comfortable he went fast asleep and never woke up till next day. Then the little ant cleaned up the mess. She was so glad that Pedro was not drowned that she did not mind it at all, but she never, never let him stir the soup again.

This Spanish folk-tale with its blend of the exotic and the familiar is a little book of quality—and of feminine quality. There is a Beatrix Potter flavour about its lively incident and its domestic and farmyard details, mixed of course with something matrimonial which is not stressed in the Peter Rabbit series. (Beatrix Potter portrays parents and children, but more often bachelor types like Messrs Jackson and Jeremy Fisher, or women who live alone like Mrs Tiggy-Winkle and Mrs Tittlemouse.) Carol shows a lively interest in weddings, and she found the ant's wedding, 'a grand wedding among the cornstalks', a peak of excitement in the story. The ant's dressing-up before her husband-hunting was another moment in the narrative where all Carol's pleasures of real life blended with those she found in a book. During the opera season early in the winter she had refused to go to sleep till she saw us both dressed in our evening clothes; indeed, whenever we go out she likes to inspect us from head to toe. Dressing-up is one of her own favourite games with Ann, and the ant therefore was a character after her own heart.

We met yet another Margaret Wise Brown text in *The Sleepy Little Lion,* with photographs by Ylla. This is a large photographic picture book about a lion cub from a zoo, who goes forth into the outside world. Actually he is in the world but not of it, for he yawns and he yawns and he finally goes to sleep. The concluding words of the book are, 'And now you go to sleep too!' As it was daytime when I read the story for the first time I didn't read this instruction. That night however Dick read the book to her in bed, and put in the final plea. At first Carol couldn't believe this was in the book; then she called me in, shaking with excitement, 'The book says Carol is to go to sleep too.'

Rather belatedly perhaps I have begun to read her poetry. I had told her about witches,

> *Double double*
> *Toil and trouble,*
> *Fire burn*
> *And cauldron bubble,*

and during these months when she has been ill she has often asked 'Please, please, do that talking the witches do.'

So I brought out *Sung Under the Silver Umbrella,* a collection of poems for young children selected by the Literature Committee of the Association of Childhood Education. We used to wear out copies of this in the children's department at Dunedin library and re-order it regularly. I thought then that it was a very special anthology, and experiences at home have confirmed the opinion. The collection of about three hundred poems is remarkable for the wide range of its sources—Humbert Wolfe, Lady Gregory, Vachel Lindsay, Victor Hugo, and

G. K. Chesterton are not to be found in every anthology for children, nor are translations from the Japanese. All this together with poems from Walter de la Mare and Eleanor Farjeon and others make the book a distinguished one.

Carol's favourites at her first reading were: Rose Fyleman's *Mary Middling Had a Pig,* Laura Richards' *Monkeys and the Crocodile,* Dorothy Baruch's *Lawn-mower,* and Christina Rossetti's

Mix a pancake,
Stir a pancake,
Pop it in the pan.
Fry the pancake,
Toss the pancake—
Catch it if you can.

Nancy Hayes' *Shiny Little House* is the one to which she responds most. Her own face seems to shine more when I read this little poem, which, to make yet another comparison with Beatrix Potter, seems to glow with domestic pride.

I'd shine all the knives, all the windows and the floors,
All the grates, all the plates, all the handles on the doors,
Every fork, every spoon, every lid and every tin,
Till everything was shining like a new bright pin.

Four verses, and they are not enough. How rarely it comes through in adult literature, this decent joy in housewifery— occasionally in Mrs Gaskell or George Eliot, but where else? Houses in English literature are many of them substantial enough; they exist but are not produced—the 'sense of process is absent'. [Since writing this I've discovered Joyce Cary's Sara.]

During all the negotiations between the two families over exchanging this flat for the new house, Carol has met and become friends with Mrs M. in Littlebourne Road. She has met Mrs M.'s grandchildren and she has heard us speak of Mrs M.'s sons. She has learned directly, and even more, indirectly, by listening in to adult conversation, that Mrs M. 'is giving us her house' where her boys have been born and bred, because they are now old enough to go away and have houses of their own. All this apparently has stirred her deeply because she has talked to me a great deal lately about mothers and girls and grandmothers and grandchildren. I can see that the poem *Shiny Little House* seems to combine her three allied interests —her joy in her own home when she watches me clean it, her pleasure in play houses, and her awakened interest in the possibility of one day having a 'real house of my very own'.

Poetry of a more traditional kind we have found in *The Baby's Opera, a Book of Old Rhymes with New Dresses,* by Walter Crane. Our copy is the original edition of 1877 engraved and printed in colours by Edmund Evans, who engraved also for Randolph Caldecott and Kate Greenaway and who by his craftsmanship made possible that first great period of English picture books. The book originally had been given not to Carol but to me, as an item for my small collection of early children's books. However in this house 'all is known, all is found'. Carol as usual found its hiding-place and brought it forth, thrilled with the sight of printed music. This has always excited her. It reminds her of next door, the 'piano room' there, and the happy occasions when Beth lets her thump away. When I told her the name of the Crane book she glowed with pleasure. 'My very own opera book!' Some of her delight in it comes from the fact that she imagines she is now sharing the pleasures of an opera season with Dick and me.

The Baby's Opera look's a period piece. I remember that when I first saw Walter Crane picture books some twelve or thirteen years ago I did not think them childlike. Most of them were out of print when I was working as a children's librarian, and with no opportunity to test their appeal with present-day children I had always believed that Crane survived as an influence on children's book illustration not as a living illustrator in the sense that Randolph Caldecott lives still. Seeing Carol's attachment to this book I am disposed to wonder at my earlier judgment. The drooping pre-Raphaelite women, like so many wives of Rossetti, are not childlike, but they appealed to my child. Perhaps that is the nub of the situation—this very quality of difference about the book from all that she has seen may explain the appeal of *The Baby's Opera* to Carol. Walter Crane's pictures enchant her. She pores over the illustrations to *Old King Cole* showing three ancient fiddlers, each odd with an oddness peculiar to each (like the 'bit' parts in British films), usually silent, with a long fixed gaze, as though she wants to take it all in, every wart and wrinkle. The pictures and music for *I Saw Three Ships* make another chosen page which she strokes gently. I have occasionally seen her do this before. Sometimes it is indication of doubt, at other times a sign that this is a beloved picture. Her favourite verse is:

> *And one could whistle and one could sing*
> *And other play on the violin,*
> *Such joy there was at my wedding*
> *On New Year's Day in the morning.*

How, I wonder, did this version come to supersede the earlier form:

> *The Virgin Mary and Christ they bare*
> *On Christmas Day in the morning.*

> *He did whistle and she did sing, she did sing, she did sing,*
> *And on all the bells on earth did ring,*
> *On Christmas Day in the morning.*

Other songs and verses she has enjoyed are *Tom, Tom the Piper's Son, Jack and Jill,* and *Rock-a-bye Baby.* These I think she accepts as plain statements of fact, pure history. *Ye Frog's Wooing* puzzled her.

> *It was the frog lived in the well,*
> *Heigh-ho! says Rowley;*
> *And the merry mouse under the mill,*
> *With a Rowley, Powley, Gammon and Spinach.*
> *Heigh-ho! says Anthony Rowley.*

She liked it, but she didn't know where she was—then one evening we had a gammon steak for dinner and her delight was lovely to watch. It is a commentary on the passing of a traditional lore that there were many songs in this collection I could not sing, and by another generation these will have vanished, in New Zealand at least, from popular knowledge. We take our folk-lore from America now. The Golden Book *Nursery Songs,* which is in hundreds of homes here now and was used as a song-book at Carol's kindergarten is two-thirds traditional English and one-third popular American. *Dame Get Up and Bake Your Pies* gives way to *Oh, Susanna.*

4 OCTOBER 1949

On 15 September we moved here to Littlebourne Road and until this afternoon Carol has had no stories. She finds herself in a dramatic new world, and books for the time being have no part in it. When the tide of packers and carriers ebbed she had a bus route and traffic to watch, and new neighbours to become acquainted with. 'What's your name?' I heard her calling. (The information is useful.) Carpet-layers, gas men, electricians, plumbers, and a gardener oddly like McGregor came fast on one another's heels. 'So many people,' she said. They climbed on roofs, mounted ladders, disappeared through man-holes in the ceiling, crawled into cupboards, banged away with their hammers at wood and piping. For one person in the house this was music and entertainment. Once the tool-bags were opened, everyone provided Carol with a different spectacle to watch. They were alike only in this, their courtesy in face of a child's questions, for she cross-examined them like a King's Counsel.

However the book world of Garfield Avenue still echoes in her play. On Sunday afternoon Jean called to see the new house. It was her first visit since I had read Carol *The Story of the Little Ant.* 'You gave me *The Little Ant,*' was Carol's greeting and she dashed away to her own room, returning ten minutes later all bedecked, hair ribbons round her ankles and wrists, and the remains of my black evening frock round her head as a mantilla.

Today was about the first time we have had the house to ourselves, when I could wash dishes or make beds unaccompanied by the sound of hammers. When Carol was finally convinced 'nobody coming today' she looked round for a substitute and fell back on her old habits. 'Let's have stories,' she said, bringing up a collection of fairy tales open at *Hot Cockalorum,* sometimes called *Master of All Masters.* This is it:

Once there was a funny-looking old gentleman who hired a girl for a servant. He told her he had something to teach her, for in his house he had his own names for everything.

'What will you call me?' he asked.

'Master or Mister, or whatever you please, sir,' she said.

'No, you must call me "master of all masters". And what will you call this?' he asked, pointing to his bed.

'Bed or couch or whatever you please, sir.'

'No, that is my "barnacle". And what do you call these?' he asked, pointing to his pantaloons.

'Breeches or trousers, or whatever you please, sir.'

'You must call them "squibs and crackers". And what do you call her?' he asked, pointing to the cat.

'Cat or kit, or whatever you please, sir.'

'You must call her "white-faced simminy". And this now,' pointing to the fire, 'What would you call this?'

'Fire or flame or whatever you please, sir.'

'You must call it "hot cockalorum". And what's this?' he went on, pointing to the water.

'Water, or wet, or whatever you please, sir.'

'No, "pondalorum" is its name. And what do you call all this?' he asked as he pointed to the house.

'House, or cottage, or whatever you please, sir.'

'You must call it "high topper mountain".'

That night the servant woke her master up in a fright and said:

'Master of all masters, get out of your barnacle and put on your squibs and crackers. For white-faced simminy has got a spark of hot cockalorum on her tail, and unless you get some pondalorum high topper mountain will be all on hot cockalorum.'

And that's the end of the story.*

I read this tale once to Carol shortly before we left Garfield Avenue and she had dissolved into helpless laughter, eyes streaming and legs in the air. Today also she was almost hysterical as the absurd patterns of sound fell on her ear. 'Whatever you please, sir,' seemed to her as funny as 'white-faced simminy'. At last I have cleared up a minor mystery, the reason for the mania, common to both Ann and Carol during our last two months at Garfield Avenue, of calling things by nonsensical names. 'Do you know what we call the builder-men? Christopher Robins'— always followed by gales of laughter.

After I read *Hot Cockalorum* she asked for *Chicken Licken*.

Nursery Book. Twenty-five old favourite tales retold by F. Cavanah. (Racine, Wisconsin. Whitman n.d.)

I had time to read the beginning only, when the doorbell rang—another invader, this time from the insurance company. The hiatus had been too good to last, but the fragment of the story had been enough to set Carol on a new track. Later in the afternoon I observed her gravely trotting off to tell the king the sky had fallen. To an adult, even to an older child, this point in the story has a touch of fantasy, even of the ridiculous about it—the hen is obviously talking 'out of her class'. Not to Carol however. Dick often talks to her about the Royal Family and the 'King's Navee', and when the royal tour was postponed he had formally notified her that His Majesty was ill and would not be visiting her as expected. Carol therefore accepts the King as an intimate part of life even if she has never seen him, much as a pious medieval peasant might accept the existence of St Anthony of Padua as part of his cosmos. On Carol's view of it, therefore, a chicken who goes off to tell the king the sky has fallen is acting in an entirely rational way.

I am now coming to discriminate between different kinds of nonsense, for what appears nonsense to an adult often makes sober sense to a child. Thus Carol accepts the majority of nursery rhymes almost gravely. *Hot Cockalorum* however was nonsense to both of us, amusing to me, but wildly mad to her. I almost envied her the experience and others like it which will follow. Happy mad writing is the rarest thing of all in adult literature; which is probably why grown men and women so often go back to the nonsense of childhood.

At dinner time tonight Carol made up her own nonsensical chant, composed of three oddly disparate elements: a remark of the carpet-layer, 'That's a classy toolbag', a derisive comment she overheard about a friend's friend 'dotty Mr Biddell', and thirdly 'white-faced simminy'. At the top of her voice, wild with excitement till her parents were wild with fury, she shrieked over and over again, 'Classy toolbag—dotty Biddell —white-faced simminy.' Long after she was in bed the maddening chant went on. It seemed hours before silence came from her room—one of those occasions when the influence of literature is much, much too overwhelming when transferred to real life.

5

Four to Four and a Half

2 NOVEMBER 1949

CAROL is four but does not know it yet, as the formal rites
have not been observed. The birthday party was postponed. More bronchitis, the worst attack to date. For two
days she lay in bed with that terrifying inactivity which makes
the very demandingness of convalescence a relief. Once the
crisis was over I was grateful for the chance to clear up the
litter she made when she cut up her paper dolls, and to take
her more books when 'I've read all that one—I want Mrs
Tittlemouse now.' The old books kept her interested for hours
at a time which was just as well, because I had no opportunity
to leave the house for a couple of weeks.

One new book she did have. This was *Three Brown Bears
and the Manpower Man* by Margaret Dunningham, with pictures by Anne McCahon. It is four years now since I first
read *Three Brown Bears*. Carol was a baby of three months,
and at that time I could not imagine her being anything more.
It simply did not occur to me when I wrote a review of it that
here was a book which we as a family might one day enjoy.

Children's literature still appeared to me as something for other people's children.

It was obvious from the moment we opened *Three Brown Bears* that Carol was going to enjoy it. The whole story with its train journey, its action centred round the Wellington wharves, and the bears' desire for a home, all this touched close to her own experience. I am glad my daughter has met her own country in print and on paper so early, for I had to wait till nine or ten before seeing any reference to New Zealand in a book—other than in school textbooks, and they of course did not really count, being without the alembic of narrative. By the time in my own childhood when books and life itself came together it was late enough for me to have come to believe that happenings worthy of print occurred only outside my own country.

Even now there is no child's picture book about Dunedin, but the Wellington of *Three Brown Bears and the Manpower Man* was near enough for Carol. A hilly town with a harbour is her idea of what a city is, and Wellington, from which our friends emerge at odd intervals, is already well established in her imagination. When the story was over she went through the book explaining it to the Bermot doll. 'Those are Wellington houses . . . that's Wellington wharves . . . that's Wellington harbour.' Then she hunted round the small sketches trying to find the water police.

There were questions about the book but not where one might have expected them. The 'manpower man' raised no query—he was accepted. Nor did the vocabulary present difficulties. She asked me what 'regulations', 'amazing', and 'polite' meant, then almost visibly stowed them away for future reference. She did complain however at the station scene, because there was no guard on the platform 'to tell the train to go', obviously remembering the incident of Lois Lenski's *Little Train*. And when the bears got into the train and were ejected from their seats she asked, 'Why can't they stay in the class carriage?' I explained that only people go in 'class' carriages. 'Have you ever seen a bear in a railway carriage, Carol?' She grinned, and I told her that cattle-trucks were not at all comfortable. 'And that's why the bears are pleased to be in the guard's van.'

These were minor points of bewilderment but she showed real signs of distress when the bears had difficulty finding a home. She wanted to turn over the pages quickly to make sure they found anchorage. The duration of this tension in the story was just long enough for her to bear comfortably.

As a postscript at the end of the story I explained, 'These aren't the same bears Goldilocks knew.' 'No,' agreed Carol, 'this is a very special kind of bear book.'

5 NOVEMBER 1949

Yesterday and again today, after I had given her an early bath and put her back in bed about four o'clock, she asked me for some poems. I brought out *Sung Under the Silver Umbrella* again and found an old copy of *A Child's Garden of Verses* which was new to her. The Stevenson was a 1919 edition, illustrated in a style of some twenty years earlier, and the pictures blended with the text as many modern illustrations do not, for *A Child's Garden of Verses* blends something of childhood which is abiding with much of another century's childhood which has gone for ever.

Our Carol lying in her bed in summer, like the child who was Stevenson ninety years before, can

Hear the grown-up people's feet
Still going past me in the street.

and resent it equally; but the world of candles and lamplighters
and aunts whose dresses rustle on the floor is far away, even
more historic than hatred of rice pudding in A. A. Milne's
verse. As a small child I lived in a house with gas lighting
and have read by hurricane lamp during farm holidays. I
heard my mother talk of lamp-lighters in Leeds when she
was a child but my Carol is a child of an all-electric age. She
has never seen a lamp that has to be lit. When we came to
Windy Nights,

> *Whenever the moon and stars are set*
> *Whenever the wind is high,*
> *All night long in the dark and wet*
> *A man goes riding by.*
> *Late in the night when the fires are out,*
> *Why does he gallop and gallop about?*

she asked, 'What's a gallop?'

The question reminded me of an incident in Roslyn town-
ship a few weeks ago when she rushed wildly from the barber's
shop to the pavement crying, 'Look Mummy, look Mummy,
look—a horse'—as strictly speaking it was, that bottleman's
spavined nag. So 'gallop' is a foreign word. Never in her
wildest dreams would Carol connect the sound of trees in
the wind with any horseman, solitary or otherwise. Although
the verse gave her pleasure this was not the same pleasure it
gave to children of another age—even to mine. We at least
saw enough of horses to be able to play that game of counting
white ones for a month.

Most of all she liked *Rain,* and

> *A birdie with a yellow bill*
> *Hopped upon my window sill.*

All was known there and could be relished without bewilderment. She knows what she wants from a poetry book. When

we came to *Where Go the Boats* I began to sing it to the tune I learned as a child but Carol became cross. 'This isn't a music book. This is poetry. You *say* it.'

I began *Sung Under the Silver Umbrella* yesterday with the familiar poems I knew she liked, Rose Fyleman's *Mice* and *Mary Middling*, Nancy Hayes' *Shiny Little House,* and Christina Rossetti's 'pancake poem' as Carol calls it. These are verses

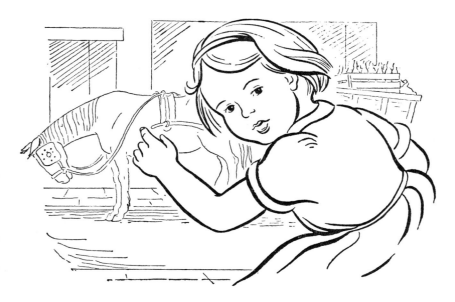

which have, since they were first heard last August, passed over into her everyday speech, sometimes in complete lines, sometimes in the odd phrase or word. I hear her talking to herself about pigs, and pancakes, and shining houses. 'Let me shine too,' she says as I polish the cedar chest. We also re-read Dorothy Baruch's *Lawn-mower,* a fairly representative poem of the American school of versifying that takes some object in which children are interested and tailors rhymes to fit. The difficulty

is of course that poetry doesn't necessarily spring into existence
that way. These verses for young children, however, do have
their moments of spontaneity, as in *The Lawn-mower:*

> *I'm the gardener to-day*
> *I push the lawn-mower*
> *Across the grass. . . .*
> *I'm the lawn's barber*
> *I'm cutting*
> *Its green hair*
> *Short.*

Like A. A. Milne's poem on the muffin man, this verse
expresses something of the three-year-old's passion for impersonation, while the fancy about the lawn's barber has the
quality of a child's imaginings. I should guess it is based on
something overheard of a child's speech. With the illustrations to this poem we ran into a difficulty typical of what
occurred several times while reading this anthology. On the
opposite page from the poem there is a decorative drawing by
Dorothy Lathrop showing a leaping child accompanied by
two geese. Carol pointed in a puzzled way at the second goose
with his bill close to the ground and said, 'That's isn't a *real*
lawn-mower?' She is not accustomed to pictures which decor-
ate: she expects illustrations which illustrate in the precise
sense of the term. I tried to explain to her that in poetry books
the 'pictures don't always match'. 'But these do,' she said,
picking up *A Child's Garden of Verses* from the bed.

And as if to disprove my theory further there was also a
mouse picture to illustrate Rose Fyleman's *Mice*. When we
came to the concluding line of this,

> *But I think mice*
> *Are nice,*

'Who thinks?' Carol asked yesterday.

'The one who wrote the poem,' I answered. She looked at me questioningly but said no more. Today when I read the poem again she repeated, when I had finished, '*I* think mice are nice.' She made it perfectly clear by her intonation that she spoke in her own voice: no poet, it was Carol White who held this opinion. Her statement and the statement in the poem were as different as lines repeated with a difference in a triolet or rondeau.

Odd the confusions of childhood. The voiced ones like 'Who thinks?' or 'That's not a real lawn-mower' are like the visible part of an iceberg, only a fragment of the greater mass below the surface. I read *The Owl and the Pussy-cat* to her yesterday, and she must have taken the expression 'elegant fowl' as a polite form of greeting, because this morning as I stood, aproned at the wash-tub, Carol said affectionately, 'Mummy, you elegant fowl.' When I laughed she looked hurt and went rather red. To a small child *The Owl and the Pussy-cat* isn't necessarily a funny poem. Carol listened to much of it in solemn stillness. The mince, the quince, and the runcible spoon, the pea-green boat, the honey and the money, these are Crusoe-like details which were accepted quite seriously. As far as Carol is concerned humour is present only in the second verse:

> And there in the wood a piggy-wig stood,
> With a ring at the end of his nose,
> > His nose,
> > His nose,
> With a ring at the end of his nose.

When they take the ring away and are married next day, Carol's grave mood returned. Marriage is a serious business. The ending for her was entirely in keeping:

They danced by the light of the moon,
The moon,
The moon,
They danced by the light of the moon.

This moon of Lear's is quite different from the nursery moon which shines in Margaret Wise Brown's story of *The Good-night Moon.* The Lear moon is sinister, like that in Llewellyn Powys's essay *Treachery in the Heavens*—'*If there had been no moon* then had the history of the human race been far different'—which I suddenly remembered as I read.*

Sharing a story with Carol stirs my memories of both childhood reading and that more recent reading of adult life. Reading to children is not something one does in a vacuum. Children's literature itself is part of the great whole of literature, and I shall always feel grateful to the professional training which made me aware of it and left me excited about it— excited in much the same way as those nineteenth century folk-lorists reared on written literature must have been when they discovered a world of poetry and prose in the peasant vernacular. For them ever afterwards, I imagine, the written and the spoken literature would illuminate one another like confronting mirrors.

13 NOVEMBER 1949

Carol had her postponed birthday party yesterday and as the house filled up with all the small girls from Garfield Avenue in their light summer dresses I began to feel that at last we had really taken root in our new house and began to inhabit it. 'What a field day this would have been for Lewis Carroll,' said Dick.

*Llewellyn Powys. *Ebony and Ivory* (Penguin Books, 1939), p 341.

14 NOVEMBER 1949

We have been reading two of the birthday Potters, *The Tale of Two Bad Mice* and *The Tale of Mr Jeremy Fisher*.

'Once upon a time there was a frog called Mr Jeremy Fisher; he lived in a little damp house amongst the buttercups at the edge of a pond.'

Carol looked at the picture and remarked, 'It's called Jeremy Fisher but I *think* it's really Mr Jackson.' (We haven't read *Mrs Tittlemouse* for months but Mr Jackson has evidently impressed her deeply.)

'The water was all slippy sloppy in the larder and in the back passage. But Mr Jeremy Fisher liked getting his feet wet; nobody ever scolded him and he never caught a cold.'

Carol purred as if to say, 'Fortunate Mr Fisher.' She was interested in all the details of Mr Jeremy's preparation for fishing and began to make comparisons with the fishermen she sees on the wharf each Sunday. When the real adventure of the story begins, I could not but admire the way in which Mrs. Potter here, as always, prepared for her denouement. When the water-beetle tweaks at the toes of Mr Jeremy Fisher dangling in the water, the author has warned her readers of disaster and hinted that her hero's position is precarious. To borrow a phrase from Rebecca West, this is striking 'a low note on a scale that is struck higher up' by Tolstoi when he creates the prophetic incident of the horse race in *Anna Karenina*. One sees a skilled novelist's technique on the scale of the Queen's Doll's House.

'A great big enormous trout came up—Ker-pflop-p-p-p! with a splash—and it seized Mr Jeremy with a snap "Ou! Ou! Ou!" and then it turned and dived down to the bottom of the pond.'

Carol accepted this dramatic disaster calmly, without any

of the dismay she showed at the disappearance of the boy's parents in *Paul Alone in the World*. I am coming to see a distinction between disasters in children's books, between those which excite and those which temporarily destroy security, the panic-creating incidents. It is the difference, to use an adult comparison, between the joyful fear of a 'cops and robbers' film, and the fear without joy which one feels in Orwell's *1984*. ('The tragic work of art which is too close to one's own experience is intolerable,' said X. on the phone the other day after seeing *Open City*.)

Be that as it may, Carol saw the swallowing of Jeremy Fisher without a tremor. 'Doesn't he like being eaten?' she asked with a mild curiosity, but she watched him disgorged with satisfaction. 'The trout was so displeased with the taste of the mackintosh that in less than half a minute it spat him out again.' She immediately turned back the pages to the beginning of the incident, but whether to discover exactly how it happened, or merely in childish pleasure I could not say.

Next I read *Two Bad Mice*. When it was finished she said, 'I love it, I love it, I love it. Again!' But I did not need to be told; I knew this as I read her the story of Tom Thumb and his Hunca Munca and the havoc they wrought. It begins, 'Once upon a time there was a very beautiful doll's house; it was red brick with white windows and it had real muslin curtains and a front door and a chimney.' And that to my mind is a very beautiful opening sentence. 'Beautiful' is used three times in this book, reminding me irresistibly on each occasion of Osbert Sitwell's cook, 'the loveliest piece of turbot . . . a beautiful saddle of lamb'.★

The triple use of 'and' (wrongly despised conjunction of the school essay) is a precise echo of children's speech, when 'ands'

★Osbert Sitwell. *Laughter in the Next Room* (Macmillan, 1949), p. 55.

are used in batches at a time with a rising inflection and value. I noticed Carol's smile as I read 'real muslin curtains'. This adjective in this context is no relation whatever to the adult 'real', a word with little meaning except possibly to philosophers—but 'real' to Carol, who is forever drawing her distinctions between 'real' and 'pretendy', is a vibrating charged word of great significance, meaning approximately the good and the beautiful and the true.

However, within the doll's house which Tom Thumb and Hunca Munca raid all is not 'real', as the two marauding mice discover. 'Jane [the doll] was the cook; but she never did any cooking, because the dinner had been bought readymade in a box of shavings. There were two red lobsters and a ham and some pears and oranges. They would not come off the plates, but they were extremely beautiful.' Aunt Barbara had given Carol such a toy dinner one Christmas, so she was quite familiar with the difficulties of the mice in their attempts to eat the paint and plaster.

Tom Thumb and Hunca Munca went upstairs and peeped into the dining-room. Then they squeaked with joy. Such a lovely dinner was laid out upon the table. There were tin spoons and lead knives and forks and two dolly chairs—all so convenient. Tom Thumb set to work to carve the ham. . . . The knife crumpled up and hurt him: he put his finger in his mouth. 'It's not boiled enough, it is hard. . . . Give me some fish, Hunca Munca.' Hunca Munca tried every tin spoon in turn; the fish was glued to the dish. Then Tom Thumb lost his temper. He put the ham in the middle of the floor, and hit it with the tongs and with the shovel—bang, bang, smash, smash! The ham flew all into pieces for underneath the shiny paint it was made of nothing but plaster!

On the second reading of this Carol laughed uproariously. The incident was her equivalent of a custard-pie movie. She had not laughed at all on the first reading, but now I come to think of it her laughs are more often than not produced on the second reading rather than the first.

Then those mice set to work to do all the mischief they could—especially Tom Thumb. He took Jane's clothes out of the chest of drawers in her bedroom and he threw them out of the top floor window. But Hunca Munca had a frugal mind. After pulling half the feathers out of Lucinda's bolster, she remembered that she herself was in want of a feather bed. With Tom Thumb's assistance she carried the bolster downstairs and across the hearth-rug. It was difficult to squeeze the bolster into the mouse-hole: but they managed it somehow.

When Hunca Munca collected a cradle, 'What's a cradle?' asked Carol. 'A bassinette for a baby,' I explained. C: 'Not a *real* bassinette like ours—no legs.' The word 'cradle' in *Rock-a-bye Baby* which she has heard dozens of times has made no impression upon her at all. The characterization of Hunca Munca is a delightful study of the eternal feminine. Infinitely less destructive than Tom Thumb, Hunca Munca is concerned mainly with collecting spoils for her own house, not unlike Carol herself who has a genius for 'liberating' articles and moving them into her own nursery households.

15 NOVEMBER 1949

Now that we are settled in the house and the workmen have gone, Carol's life is rather lonely here at Littlebourne Road. There are no other children in the street and she has consequently taken up her imaginary companions again—not the mysterious Jeejer whom she shared with Ann a year ago but an entirely new set. The personality of the Bermot doll has blossomed suddenly and she is credited with a whole range of attributes which she never possessed in the old house when Carol's social life was 'richer, vaster'. There are references now to a cloud of people, variously described by Carol as 'my girl', 'my cousin', 'my sister', and an imaginary daughter with whom I am saddled, 'your girl Josephine'. Like two women over a fence we discuss the birthday parties, picnics, behaviour, and minor sicknesses of imaginary children, till on occasion my brain almost reels, more particularly if at the same time as these domestic dialogues canter on I am making a meal. At times I can almost see the wretched Josephine. In fact I do see her. These sessions last anything from twenty minutes to half an hour. If I interrupt the pretend with a 'real' remark such as 'Please don't open that drawer Carol,' there are protests. 'I'm not Carol. I'm Rosalie's mummy.'

This afternoon we read *The Tale of Samuel Whiskers or the Roly-Poly Pudding,* another of the birthday Potter books with more intelligence regarding the family of Mrs Tabitha Twitchit, that anxious parent. 'She used to lose her kittens continually and whenever they were lost they were always in mischief. On baking day she determined to shut them up in a cupboard.'

'Why?' asked Carol. It was not a trivial question. On this and other occasions when she asks 'Why?' I find that she interrupts when the continuity of two events is not apparent. To an adult it may follow: kittens misbehave, therefore they shall be locked up. To Carol it was not a true sequence, hence the query.

The tale of Tom's adventures with the rats and his final humiliation when tied in a roll of dough, represented a more complicated plot than our usual run of stories. Carol itched to get to the pudding incident, so I skipped till we got there and she was thrilled. She seemed to have no sentimental feelings about her hero's predicament at all.

Cousin Ribby in *Samuel Whiskers* with her almost instinctive

dislike of the very young is one more notable Potter characterization. 'He's a bad kitten, Cousin Tabitha; he made a
cat's cradle of my best bonnet last time I came to tea. Where
have you looked for him?' I thought as I read of Carol's
devastating verdict on Mrs Z. 'She doesn't want any babies
—she doesn't like to get things creased.'

[The book seemed a little old for her so it was put away
and not brought out again until seven months later. See diary
entry for 22 June 1950.]

25 NOVEMBER 1949

I have read Carol only two stories during the last week,
which was a busy one for both of us. Ann came to play on
Saturday. Glorious day for Carol whose passionate excitement
at having company was rather pathetic to see. A walk to the
wharves on Sunday; Peter to play on Monday; carpet-laying
on Tuesday; the Summer Show on Wednesday; plumbers and
electricians on Thursday; and gardening on Friday.

Her visit with Dick to the Summer Show was obviously
measured by Carol against the child's outing in Marion
Conger's *Circus Time*. 'I didn't see a lady swallow a rattle-
snake.'

During the last ten days or so, when the chance offered, I
have been making rough jottings of any references to the
books she has read. These occur all the time although I don't
always have the opportunity to write them down. The notes
below are mainly kitchen conversations when I pretend I'm
writing on the grocery list.

From the kitchen window yesterday I saw her toy broom
sticking up among the cabbages and I asked her to bring it
inside. She protested: 'That's Mr McGregor's scarecrow to
keep the birds away.' A few minutes later she has forgotten

about this and begins to tell me an involved story about sailing round the world and going fishing. 'I'm the conductor, Mummy.' It is a barely recognizable retelling of the *Three Brown Bears and the Manpower Man*.

Although I had once more removed the Crane *Baby's Opera* from her bookcase, she again found it and yesterday brought it up, her face set in reproach. 'You said children don't go to the opera.' 'Well, they don't.' She pointed on the back cover where there is a picture of two very small people in tails and long dress. Triumphant she pointed. 'These have got *concert clothes* on.'

I heard another echo of the Crane book in a conversation which developed from her question, 'How do you make flour?' I explained as well as I could how flour was ground in a mill, and then I took her to the front door and showed her the turretted house on the ridge opposite, which had been a mill in the old days when bullocks not buses travelled on Littlebourne Road.

Carol stared and gasped. 'The miller used to live there?' she asked. 'Yes.' 'And did he have a mummy?' 'Yes.' 'I know, a miller-mummy.' She laughed gleefully over this, then asked her last question. 'And is there "a merry mouse under the mill?" '

At other times she demands books which I have long ago returned to the library. 'I used to have a Toby book.' [*Toby's House*, see 20 July and 14 November 1948.] Or again, 'That animal book, you know.' I mention the Babar stories and several of the Golden Books, but it is clear from her expression that I am wide of the mark. 'No,—peanuts—giving peanuts —and a paper hat.' Then I have it—the Ets book *In the Forest* which we read last June when she was sick. 'You mean I went for a walk in the forest?' 'That's the one, I want it.'

Here I slide into my routine explanation about other boys and girls wanting to read the library books, knowing as I speak that this is not a really adequate reply to a young child with a sudden fresh vision of pictures she wants to look at once more. They need to own their books at this age, but few if any of the American picture books in the library can be bought in our shops, and even many of the English ones are only stocked intermittently by booksellers—a feast at Christmas and a famine during the rest of the year. Beatrix Potter's alone are always regularly in stock.

Even Potters are not ideal with every child on every occasion. In fact I have three Potter failures to record—at least failures with one particular child in one particular environment. *Ginger and Pickles* can be dismissed briefly. The plot hinges on the matter of 'credit' at a village shop, a situation beyond Carol's understanding. The difficulty with *The Tale of Mr Tod* and *The Tale of Jemima Puddleduck* was a matter of geography: the two stories are rural English and Carol is urban New Zealand. There is a passage in Nancy Mitford's *Pursuit of Love* which reminds me of these particular Beatrix Potter books and their portrayals of the wilder, almost jungle aspect of the 'peaceful English countryside'.

At Alconleigh the cruel woods crept right up to the house: it was not unusual to be awoken by the screams of a rabbit running in horrified circles round a stoat, by a strange and awful cry of the dog-fox, or to see from one's bedroom window a live hen being carried away by a vixen; while the roosting pheasant and the waking owl filled every night with wild primeval noise. In the winter when snow covered the ground, we could trace the footprints of many creatures. These often ended in a pool of blood, a mass of fur or feathers bearing witness to successful hunting by the carnivores.[*]

[*]Nancy Mitford. *Pursuit of Love* (Hamish Hamilton, 1945), p. 17.

Saki describes the same thing in his story *The Peace of Mowsle Barton*. It all seems as foreign to us as a legendary Russia with a troika driver throwing passengers to the wolves. Here at Littlebourne Road we live on the edge of a reserve of native bushland with never an animal heard or seen, and Carol therefore has no background whatever to enable her to enjoy *Mr Tod*. Too much had to be explained: why the rabbits couldn't bear the fox, for example. With *Jemima Puddleduck* I had to explain about the laying and hatching of eggs, and in both stories the dead weight of information necessary before we could get on with the story killed the pleasure. I skipped hastily to the end of each and put the books away for a year or two.

This afternoon we read Penelope Gibbon's *Riki the Eskimo*, a simple story of an Eskimo boy who takes a spear to his father at a distant fishing ground and returns home to a family feast in the igloo that evening. Carol had plenty of background for the story—the polar scenes of the magic cave last year seemed quite fresh in her mind; she has a bookish knowledge of bears, and she has been inside the canoe at the museum. Her questions were largely concerned with the gaps in her knowledge. Thus she was curious about the windows in the igloos and puzzled why the Eskimos should have no glass. She could not understand why the boy travelled in his canoe while the dogs and the sleigh went by land. I couldn't answer her. Some of the colour printing in the book was clumsy and confused us both.

Riki is an outline story much less detailed in its telling than *Mrs Tittlemouse* for example, where the camera eye moves in with a sharp focus. I think that Carol likes detail in a story about an environment similar to her own; in a book with an exotic or foreign background a broader sweep is required. This is the direct opposite of the adult's requirements. Personally

with a New Zealand story, a John Reece Cole for example,
I don't require any elaborate background detail; with a Euro-
pean novel I welcome every detail given.

Pelle's New Suit, by Elsa Beskow, was the second choice.
In this story, translated from the Swedish, the young hero
literally earns his clothes. Pelle clips his lamb, and in exchange
for errands and help on farm and garden has the wool carded
and spun, woven and dyed, and made into a suit. Much of
this was as foreign to Carol as any Eskimo with kayak and
sleigh. Pelle watering a garden, weeding carrots, and feeding
a baby was the familiar stuff of home, but 'Why is he doing
that,' she asked as Pelle took shears to his lamb. Only yesterday she was in trouble for clipping the playroom carpet with
her scissors. She was astonished to learn that wool for clothes
came from sheep. It has never occurred to Dick or me to
explain this fact of life. (Only recently too she asked if eggs
grew on trees.)

The story is often mentioned as a good moral lesson on mut-
ual aid, and I have praised it myself in some such terms. At this
moment I am less convinced of the 'morality' of such a moral.
The 'I'll-do-something-for-you-if-you-do-something-for-me'
lesson seems hardly worth learning. It is on a level with 'I'll
love you if you are good'. An argument might be advanced
that this is identical with the teaching of many traditional fairy
stories, where the young brother who helps the old man or
the old woman is invariably rewarded. There is this difference,
however, that the character in such stories usually helps because
he is good-natured—the magic reward is made long after the
deed of helping is done.

10 DECEMBER 1949

At four, Carol's interest in the everyday world has not

abated one jot, even if that wide-eyed awe and stare so char-
acteristic at two years has disappeared. She regards the here
and now with the same relish as of old but she is prepared
to go beyond it, to accept different ways of doing things from
what is familiar at home. She is making comparisons. Indeed,
throughout childhood there goes on a quiet observation of
other households, which vary enormously one from another
even in a homogeneous country like this. Certainly they differ
to a child who brings the needle eye of the anthropologist
to the observation of social life. The cooking and serving of
food, hygiene, temperament, the leisure activities of parents,
all are noted and compared. 'Beth sings when she is cooking',
or 'Cynthia uses a jug when she washes hair', or 'Mrs X.
doesn't let children pick flowers.'

From this continual appraisal and comparison, Carol is
coming gradually to have some notion of the world's variety,
some awareness of 'other rooms, other voices'. It has all been
preparatory for her enjoyment of books about other countries;
she has met minor differences between living habits before she
encounters major ones. At all events I have felt for some time
that she was old enough to appreciate my favourite among
picture books, Thomas Handforth's *Mei Li,* that magnificent
and lovingly made story of Pekin children. She has been interested in China all the year, ever since I gave her a green coolie
hat, my last remaining piece of tourist loot from Honolulu.
She has asked dozens of questions about it—where it came
from, why it was such a shape, who used to wear it. Although
the hat has been lost ever since the removal, the interest which
it aroused has not slackened. I noticed the other week her
sudden excitement when, looking through the pages of an old
Life, she came across pictures of Chinese peasants in coolie
hats like the one I had given her. Gradually, without any

particular effort on anybody's part she has built up her own picture of China, an askew portrait perhaps—odd hats, rice, beautiful vases, and living on rivers—but I am sure that to her it all has a deeply felt reality none the less.

The environment of Mei Li's story is alien, but the opening of the book leads a child out into the strange world from a point which is on familiar ground. While her mother bakes, Mei Li is dusting and scrubbing and sweeping the house—her duty as a Chinese girl, be it noted, not a 'pretend'. Later the girl slips away from home to follow her brother to a New Year's fair in the walled city of Pekin. The text is simple and clear, and the pictures, black and white lithographs, are aesthetically satisfying to an adult and miraculously clear to a child. Words and pictures run parallel—there is no hiatus. There in pictures are the bridge, the people in rickshaws, the men on shabby mongrel ponies, the beggar girl, and the high city gate.

When Mei Li joined her brother on the frozen canal and the children travelled over ice on sleds, I reminded Carol of the Santa Claus sleigh and that sledge Riki had driven in the Eskimo book. She was deeply interested in all this, as she was throughout the reading of the story, although it was longer and more demanding on her comprehension than any book she had previously met. Almost visibly she was trying to take it in. For the most part too, she accepted it. Although Mei Li and her friends wore strange clothes, Carol accepted them as children like herself, not as funny people.

Two things however did distress her—one momentarily, one, I expect, more permanently. There is a reference in the text to the more restricted life of Chinese girls. Mei Li was not really supposed to go away to the fair. 'Why does Mei Li have to stay home?' I explained how it was in China, but she would not admit the fairness of the arrangement. 'You let me go to the museum—why can't they in China?' At dinner tonight however she announced to me that she wouldn't go to school next year after all. 'You can bake and I'll do the work.' Then she proposed a detailed programme of housewifery, which was a recapitulation of all Mei Li's tasks in her Chinese home.

Her bewilderment over the beggar girl will be less easily unravelled. During the reading, during her bath, during dinner and again as she was going to bed, Carol asked question after question about this character. 'Why did the beggar girl need money? Where was her father? Why didn't he give her some?' The whole plight of the child came as a shock. Carol went to sleep after telling me of her pious intention to give the beggar girl her best toys.

Whereas Carol's enjoyment with *Mei Li* was comparable to that of an intelligent young woman among people more sophisticated than herself, her enjoyment of *That Baby*, by L. Frank, could be likened to that of a person at a social gathering of her contemporaries, completely at ease and unpuzzled by her surroundings. *That Baby* is one of the sanest books I have come across on the subject of a child's relationship with a newcomer into the family circle. A note on the back of its title-pages gives an acknowledgment to Anna Freud and Dorothy Burlingham for their permission to take photographs for the book at the Hampstead Nursery, but the author, one would guess, owes something more profound to those distinguished women. Nevertheless, the great virtue of the book is not so much this debt to contemporary psychology as the complete realism it shows, the awareness of the problems of everyday life—all this on a human, not an academic plane. The pictured mother in the story sorting over a drawer of old baby clothes while her first-born watches, is a frankly pregnant-looking woman, a little weary and finely drawn about the face; even her hair has the lack-lustre look of late pregnancy. After the second child is born *That Baby* recreates the rather desolate state of any child at this period of family life, when the mother is constantly absenting herself to feed the other one, when friends in the street concentrate their attention on pram occupant and cruelly ignore the elder. There was no question but that Carol felt the book keenly—and so did I.

Her first spoken response came at a passage after Peter has been told by his father that he will have a brother.

Book: Peter ran to Mummy. 'Is it really true?' he asked. He could hardly believe it because there had always been just Mummy and Daddy and Peter and now it would be different.
Carol: 'And the kittens, they live there.'
Book: 'Yes,' said Mummy, 'it is really true.' 'But will you still like me?' said Peter.

Carol at this point roared with happy laughter.

Book: 'Of course I will,' said Mummy. 'Look at Bess and her kittens. Don't you think she likes them all and looks after them all?'
Carol (still laughing): 'He thought his mummy wouldn't like him. That's a joke.'

The response, 'And the kittens they live there', is probably a very typical response at this age. I recall hearing how L., an only child, said to her mother, 'It's a bit lonely with just you and Daddy and me and the dolls.' Carol always insists that we are a 'five family'. Bermot doll is the fifth.

16 DECEMBER 1949

The reading of *That Baby* has had its carry-over into real life. The playroom is now described by Carol as the nursery,

English style; dinner has become supper. [Supper was eventually dropped but the playroom remained a nursery ever after.] Two days ago after the evening meal she said, 'I'll go off to the nursery now and play with my toys like Peter.' In ten minutes she was back. 'I don't want to play with my toys, I've been playing with them all day.' Both remarks were a direct crib from *That Baby*.

Davy's Day by Lois Lenski, like *That Baby*, is about everyday life, but everyday life shorn of any stress whatever. Davy wakes and brushes his teeth, dresses himself, and eats his breakfast. The only critical point in the narrative is cod-liver oil, and this he swallows with aplomb. Carol grinned mischievously at this juncture and pointed out truthfully enough that she did not take hers. [She made no attempt to copy the book child in this instance. She responds only to such propaganda as suits her own convenience.] The book is really at a three-year-old level, not that Carol's enjoyment is lessened on that account. She is familiar with every stick of experience in it, and smiles radiantly while I read; then, 'Do it again.'

We have read *Herbert the Lion* twice now, and Carol often chooses this to look at in bed after dinner. This, the first children's book by Clare Newbery who is so much better known for her stories and pictures about cats, is vaguely reminiscent of magazine illustrations of the 1920's. It has a period flavour now. Wholly fantastic by adult standards, from the child's viewpoint this tale apparently is sober realism. Carol saw nothing odd in keeping a lion as a pet; and, indeed, once this situation is accepted, the story is rational enough.

Sally the heroine keeps a lion who, well disposed towards the human race, rather overdoes it. This Herbert is too friendly and his displays of affection scare the wits out of everyone. He proves an insuperable obstacle to the family's social intercourse.

Pretty soon the postman stopped bringing the letters to Sally's house, he was so afraid of poor Herbert, and the butcher's boy stopped bringing the meat, and the milkman stopped bringing the milk, and the grocer stopped bringing the groceries, and all of Sally's friends stopped coming to see her, and her grandmother and grandfather and all her aunts and uncles and cousins stopped coming.

This to Carol spelled tragedy, and her face puckered until the story moved logically forward. Sally's parents decided to move out west where the lion might be better accommodated —the obvious step to take. We too had moved house better to accommodate a new baby.

I noticed on the second reading that Carol pointed to three pictures of Herbert in three sizes, 'He grew and he grew and he grew', with a slightly harder thump each time. Two years ago, or even one, there would have been difficulty in accepting these three pictures as the same lion at different stages.

21 DECEMBER 1949

Dick has bought *Little Black Sambo*. Here once again one notices the exquisite use of 'and'.

And Black Mumbo made him a beautiful little red coat and a pair of little blue trousers. And Black Jumbo went to the bazaar and bought him a beautiful green umbrella and a lovely little pair of purple shoes with crimson soles and crimson linings.

Carol listened to this with real awe, a different response from the easy acceptance of *Davy's Day* and different too from the response to *That Baby,* when all her deepest feelings were involved. Black Sambo represents drama to Carol: after all he is threatened many times with being eaten alive, definitely adventure by any standards. Yet there was no terror as she listened, and I have been wondering why. Is it because the story begins with Little Black Sambo in security? His mother and father are there, solid, before any tigers appear on the scene. After this adventure, the hero is back in security. 'And they all sat down to supper. And Black Mumbo ate 27 pancakes, and Black Jumbo ate 55, and Little Black Sambo ate 169 because he was so hungry.'

The story is an adventure, not a nightmare. In an adventure the principal character goes forth from security to insecurity and back to port; a nightmare is an adventure without a port. *Paul Alone in the World* by this criterion is nightmare, and so of course are many modern novels. The film, *Dead of Night,* owed much of its terror to precisely this absence of port.

We read the book once four days ago. This morning she came into my bed and said, 'I'm little Black Sambo and you are the tiger and you say I'm going to eat you all up.' So at the crack of dawn we went through the story. She gave me blue trousers and a red coat, prompted me to tie a knot in my tail to carry the green umbrella, but finally became rather muddled by the purple shoes with crimson soles and crimson linings.

'Things have to be imagined to tell,' Walter de la Mare says somewhere. Little Black Sambo had told.

That Baby is much in her thoughts. She insists on using a knife and fork 'like Peter'. When I was cooking, she asked 'Can I lick this clean like Peter in the story?' There was a reference, too, to *Bad Mousie*. 'Bermot doll, if you are naughty I'll send you to the Night Owl.'

25 DECEMBER 1949

This afternoon in the sun on the upper lawn at Littlebourne I read Carol some of her Christmas books while Victoria rolled on the grass. In the deep midsummer heat the baby alone had the energy to move. In the houses on the ridge blinds were pulled down. We could hear no footsteps in the street, only the cool sound of a hose playing next door. Even the harbour was as deserted as the city. For the first time I knew what 'wine dark sea' meant; we could see it purple-black below the belt of bush.

All in all it was an odd experience in this almost empty world to read Carol her latest Golden Book, *The Taxi That Hurried,* about a mother and child rushing to catch a train through crowded New York streets.

It was a smart little taxi. For it could start fast—jerk—whizz! It could tear along the streets—whizz—squeak. It could stop fast—squeak—jerk. Its driver's name was Bill. He could step on the gas fast.

This is a book which has grown from its environment—and what an environment! It reminded me of nightmare rushes to railway stations in America over ten years ago, but it had little relevance to Carol's existence. Our taxis are more leisurely, with time in the briefest journey for us to discuss the driver's families and gardens, their holidays up country, or the news of the town. On Sundays, after their walk, Dick and Carol will sit for a quarter of an hour at the gate talking to Mr. F. or listening to the radio in his taxi. As far as we are concerned a story about a taxi that hurried is slightly out of this world.

Polly and Jane's Houses by Helen and Margaret Binyon was a different matter. Whereas the tensions in the other book arose from a taxi's plight among jammed traffic, the tensions in this story arise from a clash between the children's world and the adult one. Two little girls, after the manner of their kind, like to play house. They make a pillow house in their bed and are told to get up; they make a new house under the table but someone wants to sweep there; they play shops with a basket of vegetables, but these are required for dinner. When they play with some bricks the bricklayer sends them packing, and as the final tragedy a load of wood is dumped over their doll's feast in a shed. At last the grandmother understands their plight and makes Polly and Jane a house of their very own with sacking and beansticks. Carol, as I read, felt it deeply. (Her fury if her house in the playroom is disturbed is prodigious. 'I'm very angry with you.') 'Naughty bricklayers,' she remarked. Literature again had confirmed life, because the bricklayers working next door had been the one group of tradesmen who were disagreeable to the children. Their threat to chop Carol's head up still occasionally disturbs her when she remembers it.

10 JANUARY 1950

Last month's stories now echo in all her play. Daily life seems an echoing green, sounding with remarks from the books we have read together. Thus old-style dolls' tea-parties have given way to 'feasts' based on *Polly and Jane's Houses,* with leaves and flowers arranged as small banquets. We talk a great deal about Polly and Jane, and Molly and Polly from the earlier *Let's Play House.* 'Where do they live? When can we go and see them?' With so many of our intimate family friends moving about the globe, Carol half expects us to go voyaging any day.

That Baby has reverberated less happily. When told by his mother about a new brother, Peter in that book asks 'Will you still like me?', a question which made Carol laugh cheerfully at the time. Since then, however, on several occasions when I've looked cross or more often merely absent-minded, she has asked, 'Do you like me?' It appears to be asked as a genuine question not as play-acting. Since she never asked any such question before, I am curious to know whether the book has disturbed her by raising doubts not previously entertained or whether it has released some hitherto unspoken concern

into speech. [On 31 January I noted that the question had ceased and I have no recollection of its recurrence since.]

A month has passed since the reading of *Mei Li*, but she is constantly with us. I find Carol sitting on the steps in the sun or in bed in the evening with the book open at Handforth's magnificent black lithographs. This story works like a yeast in her conversation and play. The butter boxes she has in her room will suddenly cease to be shops or houses and be trans-mogrified into the city gate which has captured her imagination. 'Quickly, the city gates are closing,' she called this morning as I hesitated in the garden by the macrocarpa arch. The plight of the beggar girl in the story still disturbs her. Poverty has a fabulous quality to a present-day New Zealand child. Carol certainly cannot comprehend it fully. She never impersonates the beggar girl in her play-acting.

I have been reading her *Snippy and Snappy*, Wanda Gag's story of two field-mice who leave their usual haunts and investigate the inside of a big house in a quest for cheese. To my complete astonishment Carol found the story hilariously funny. The mice, like savages in civilization or civilized man among savages, lose their bearings in the house they enter and make absurd mistakes about the furniture and equipment of the household. Mop, lamp, and footstool are confusedly taken to be plants and trees. There is certainly a delightful absurdity about it all, but I couldn't see what Carol saw, an *intense* funniness. At such moments I feel separated from my daughter by some unbridgeable gulf.

The only problems which arose in the story were these. In one picture, a child's hand is shown picking up a ball, and as Carol still feels that where the picture ends reality ends too, she could not grasp the fact that the hand belonged to someone outside the picture. Similarly she was worried by pictures of a mouse's tail disappearing into a hole. How well suited to the child-mind is Victorian art: all is there within the frame.

Last night we were reading *The Elephant Child*, an American edition of Kipling's story, with pictures by Feodor Rojankovsky. These are not among the artist's best work, although the reproduction may be at fault here, as the book is a mass-produced article for the chain-store market. However, one very good point about the book is that the incidents chosen for illustration are those which a child might misunderstand through a failure to visualize the scene. With her memories of picture books and circuses (Carol knows more of elephants than of cows) my daughter is familiar with wild animals, but I doubt whether she could summon up *quickly* before her mind's eye the sequence of animals mentioned in Kipling's pages—elephant, ostrich, hippopotamus, giraffe. I have nothing she has said to support my guess, but I imagine her state might be like mine when, rather bemused, I listen to masculine conversation about golf, economics, or artillery. In these unfamiliar fields one's mind and imagination work too slowly to take in the sense from the flow of words. The voices race on so much more quickly than do the pictures in the mind. Spoken poetry, to people unfamiliar with it, probably presents the same difficulties. I doubt whether Carol, without Rojankovsky's explicit pictures, could have imagined a crocodile pulling an elephant's nose, or a snake pulling an elephant by the hind-leg.

Again, she can understand what is happening in a mechanical sense and still not comprehend fully. Thus she did not see why the elephant's child should be spanked for asking questions; in the legal code she is familiar with this is not an indictable offence. Even more was she baffled when later in the story the elephant's child returns and spanks his relations. 'Why?' 'Because they had spanked him,' I replied. There was a long brooding silence at this, none of the immense satisfaction shown by Neta's class when she asked for their comments.

[Ten years ago I asked a friend who was teaching a class of Standard 3 and 4 girls (aged 9-11) to collect some comments on *The Elephant's Child,* which was their favourite story at that time. Nine of the twenty-five children were attracted by the idea of retribution. 'I like it because of the spanking bits, and I think they mean his relations deserve to be spanked,' was the tenor of nine replies.]

C (appearing suddenly before me in the bathroom): How do you make things?

D: What things?

C: Babies and poems and things like that?

D (firmly): You make babies in your tummy and poems in your head.

[This and related questions has concerned her on and off all the month. She began to ask a week ago, 'How do poems get out?' I had explained about babies earlier, so I told her, 'You talk poems out of your mouth.' 'That's not getting out,' said Carol. This poetry business is less poetic than it sounds; she also asks eternally who makes veal, beef, 'chicken-meats', and so on.]

16 JANUARY 1950

We are reading the d'Aulaire picture book, *Too Big*. It is a much shorter story than most books she has now, but, as I realized over *Davy's Day,* although Carol is able to concentrate on a longer book she also enjoys brief stories which make no intellectual demands, just as the average adult enjoys a light novel much below his capacity. Minds, like elastic, don't thrive on eternal stretching. Barbara had brought the book home from the library, not knowing that when Carol was two and a half we had tested it and found it wanting. I was interested to see what my daughter would make of it after this lapse of time, particularly since she has caught up with the key situation of the story—growing too big for your clothes. She is fully aware now of growing up and out of: skimpy dresses and shrunken woollens are put on one side for Victoria. She talked about this as we read.

However, all the minor inconsistencies of the story which

worried us before were still apparent at this later reading. Carol rebelled when I read 'too big to lift the cat by the tail'. 'But big boys do that.' Or again, the book says 'He couldn't ride on the horse because he was too big—and so was the horse.' As Carol pointed out, he was too little to ride on the horse.

'Never mind,' said the little boy, 'I'll grow bigger and bigger and when I grow up I'll ride an elephant.' This on the other hand did make sense because it fits in with the sort of boasting Carol resorts to at the moment. 'I'm a builder. I built eleventeen houses with bricks, real bricks for people to live in, real people. I make houses for real people all the days.'

Yesterday she found two children in the corner of one picture.

C: What are they doing?
D: Looking at the boy on the elephant.
C: That's not a boy, that's a man.
D: That's the little boy when he grows up.

Although the pictures have shown the boy growing she doesn't connect them up as one and the same, whereas she had grasped the idea of Herbert the lion growing bigger and bigger. It may have been the embodiment in pictures of an expressed wish which confused her again; or, on second thoughts, it may be this: a lion growing bigger remains a lion, but a boy becoming a man is a substantial change which could be more difficult to grasp.

We have been re-reading *The Little Ant*. Last night she concentrated her attention most particularly on the ant's wedding. I explained about the wedding dress, the long train, and the bridesmaids.

She has taken a fancy to Deverson and Lampitt's *The Map*

That Came to Life, an informative book planned to teach older children how to read and interpret maps. Coloured illustrations showing panoramic sweeps of English countryside are placed side by side with corresponding survey maps which record the same geographical features with symbol and diagram. It is an ingenious teaching device, quite beyond Carol at the present time of course. She was interested in the landscapes alone. *The Map That Came to Life* is pure picture book to her and I can guess the reason for its appeal. The world of this book, allowing for some differences in architecture, looks not unlike the world as Carol sees it from the top lawn at Littlebourne—houses, hedges, massed trees, a spread of earth and sky, the sight of water.

She carries the book around with her a lot these days, examining it as if through a microscope. 'What is this book *about?*' she asked. 'Oh, a boy and a girl who go for a walk in England,' I answered. She hunts round the pictures and puts her finger on the children, then, doubtfully, 'This book's not *real* England!' 'It's about England, Carol.' 'Yes, but not *real* England, just paper England.'

The same panoramic quality which appealed to her in this book was part of the attraction of Robert McLoskey's *Make Way for Ducklings,* although there were other elements in this which were close to her own experience—the setting of the story, Boston's Botanical Gardens, city traffic, a kindly policeman. [On Sundays Dick and Carol often call at a suburban police-station to say 'hello'.] This is a good book for a city child. Again the theme of parents and children, even in duck and drake dress, is one which always appeals to her. Here the mallard ducks of the story are looking for a home for their young. Both of us liked the ending of the book: 'Night falls and they go to sleep.' What a satisfactory close to a

child's story this makes. It's as final as, 'He died and the
empire fell', with the implied cheerfulness of 'happy ever after.'

My favourite among the Christmas books is one Constance
gave her, *My Mother Is the Most Beautiful Woman in the World,*
a folk-tale which illustrates an old Russian proverb: we do
not love people because they are beautiful, but they seem
beautiful to us because we love them. Marfa and Ivan work
in the corn-fields and six-year-old Varya follows after them.
She gets lost, and later, trying to tell strangers who her mother
is, can only say that her mother is the most beautiful woman
in the world. All the beauties of the village are brought to
the child and Varya claims none of them. When the mother
finally appears she is squat and ugly. I don't know that Carol
appreciated the point of this at all. The parts of the story she
appeared to like most were the festival scene with girls in
dancing dresses, and Varya with her mother baking in the
kitchen. Immediately I finished reading she said, 'Let's play
Varya.' She picked up corn, she made bread, and danced and
said, 'My mother is the most beautiful woman in the world.'

Once or twice lately after a reading, she has wanted to play
the story immediately, not waiting an hour or two as formerly.
This immediate demand to act is quite new.

17 JANUARY 1950

I have borrowed McDonald's *Little Island* from the library
again. Eighteen months ago when the book was first brought
home Carol was too young to enjoy it. This time I could see
from the moment the story began that she had grown up to it.

> *There was a little island in the ocean*
> *Around it the winds blew*
> *And the birds flew*
> *And the tides rose and fell on the shore.*

Clouds passed over it,
Fishes swam round it,
And the fog came in from the sea
And hid the little island
In a soft wet shadow.

This book is one of the most beautiful picture books I know. The pictures have a stereoscopic depth: there is light and space in them, a little like Holling C. Holling's pictures in *Paddle in the Sea*. The words are clear and simple and clean to the taste and I like reading them. Some of this reader's pleasure is, I suppose, communicated. One can't tell. Anyway Carol listened happily. She brings more experience to the story now, particularly in tiny things, as I realized when she smiled and stroked the spiders and strawberries in one of the pictures. Here at Littlebourne she has picked strawberries growing in her own garden and seen the spider webs in the old shed. And in the book as now at home there were banks of flowers. Garfield Avenue was lawns and shrubs, fewer of the flower-beds which have been a real joy to her this summer in the new house.

These pleasures of recognition were not all. She was exploring in the story as well, going further. She wanted all the details about the lobsters of *Little Island* losing their shells. 'What do lobsters eat?' Then a lobster on his back catches her eye. 'Look, a bare tummy.'

I read on: 'And the seals came barking from the south to lie on the sunny rocks and raise their baby seals.'

C: What does 'raise' mean?
D: Helping baby seals to grow big and giving them food and looking after them.
C: You raise me?

I agree, and she looks through the page. We pair off mothers and fathers.

C: Is that a mother?
D: Yes.
C (accusingly): Where's her baby?
D (firmly): Hidden.

A picture of nightfall on the island's coast attracted her. She began to talk about England. 'Little boats like that go to England. I've seen them at my wharf.'

Under the sea she found a starfish and asked what a shell was. The sunset puzzled her and I realized that in both the places where we have lived the setting sun is hidden by high trees. Part of the fun of reading together is discovering the curious lacunae in her experience. I discovered she didn't know sunsets with the same surprise that B. felt when he found that the children in his country school did not know what a grocer's shop was.

She found the story exciting too.

> Then came the storm
> The wind blew from the south-east,
> Waves as big as glassy mountains
> Came before it.
> And lightning and thunder
> And always the howling whistling wind.
> And then the storm passed
> And left the little island where it found it
> In the summer sea.

The Little Island, as a book, was made with that same delight Handforth had in the making of Mei Li. I was interested to read over the illustrator's speech when he accepted the Caldecott medal for his book in 1947:

The pictures for *The Little Island* and Golden McDonald's text grew right up out of the water. This is a real little island off the coast of Maine belonging to a group of other little islands, called Vinalhaven. I saw this island grow tall or squat as the tides rose and fell. I've watched the mists blow in and hide the little island, sometimes leaving only the pine tree tops exposed hanging in space. I've rowed to and from the little island with the seals swimming just below the surface of the water; I've seen the sun rise and make a golden island for just five seconds in an early morning sea.*

31 JANUARY 1950

We have returned to more of the old pastures, with *The Story of Babar*. She has always enjoyed the de Brunhoffs' pictures, but earlier I had found the text rather elaborate. Then the book needed constant adaptation, now it seems to have the tone and vocabulary of so much of our conversation together. Moreover Carol herself has now shared in some of Babar's adventures—has been to a professional photographer, for example, a character who meant nothing to her when we read about him before. The old lady who showers Babar with gifts reminded Carol instantly of Mrs O'D., who gave her a delirious morning shopping for presents shortly before Christmas.

However in the latter pages of the book, when Babar and his Celeste return to the jungle from the big city, we ran into one capital difficulty. The old king of the elephants dies from eating mushrooms, and there is a picture of him lying well and truly dead. After this another picture of the wrinkled elderly elephants greeting Babar. Carol protested, 'But they are dead.' She turned back the page to compare the picture again with that of the dead king, and I saw her point at his

*Leonard Weisgard, in *Horn Book Magazine*, July 1947, p. 287.

wrinkled trunk. She had noticed young Babar's trunk was smooth and had assumed that the wrinkles represented the quality of deadness in elephants. It was a minute or two before I could convince her that there was only one demise.

Luckily this was soon all forgotten in her joy over Babar's wedding, which de Brunhoff describes with the detail of a bride's mother writing to friends overseas. The buying of clothes, the wedding itself, the dancing, and the band had Carol wreathed in smiles. She wore the face she wears if I tell her we are going to the beach, the transfigured look. She was a little concerned to find Queen Celeste and King Babar had no bridesmaids, an element of wedding ceremonial she has come to expect after reading *The Little Ant* and seeing the wedding at St Paul's the other morning. I explained that one had to allow for some differences with elephants.

The little ant's wedding is still a regular pantomime. She comes out of her room holding a bunch of marigolds and geraniums and dressed in a rather sepulchral veil made from my black dress; then a moment later, with one of those rapid changes of sex, like Mrs Woolf's Orlando, she plays Pedro: 'Little ant how smart you are, will you marry me?' The interest in weddings and marriage is probably common to all small girls. Katrina told me about the flower-girl at her own wedding, a four-year-old who seemed to feel she was in a fairy tale. This is a theme someone should make into a picture book, certainly it is a serious interest with Carol. She also likes to hear about girls becoming mothers and mothers becoming grandmothers. Dick and I were both amused with a talking game she played one Sunday evening after tea. Leaving no one out she paired off all her friends into married couples, the two-year-old girls with two-year-old husbands, the older sisters of four and five with more elderly spouses up to six years of age. It was a neat and thorough piece of planning. 'I think I'll take X,' she said, and even to my eye X was the pick of the bunch. 'Did *you* go into town and see all the people and choose Daddy?' 'She did,' interposed Dick. There are frets attached to all this, moments of deep panic. 'There won't be any houses left for me when I grow up and want one', or, in a lower emotional key, 'There won't be any little girls when Vicky and me are grown up.'

The theme of mothering and fathering interests her in all her stories, even when it is only incidental to a plot, as with the seals in *The Little Island;* but as I had discovered the other day she doesn't want the subject wholesale. We were reading *Over in the Meadow,* a modern illustrated version of an old nursery song, which goes:

Over in the meadow where the stream runs blue
Lived an old mother fish and her little fishes two. . . .
Over in the meadow in a hole in a tree
Lived an old mother owl and her little owls three.

and so on up to 'Old mother beaver and her little beavers ten'. Carol listened with a very dull face, then closed the book with a snap. 'I don't like that story.' When I asked her why, she couldn't tell me at first, but at length she said, 'Too much mothers and too many babies.'

'Acting grown-ups' is a favourite game with her. She has a drawer of dressing-up clothes in her room, but what she likes most are the occasions late in the evening when I fling gloves, cape, and scarf on the sofa and leave them there till next morning. Then she gets up early and robes herself, coming triumphant to our room before we are up. 'Look, I'm real grown-up real.'

That of course is quite self-conscious acting, yet sometimes she can fall into it swiftly and quietly, so that one is barely aware that a transition from real to pretend has been made. Thus during the past two weeks since we read *My Mother Is the Most Beautiful Woman in the World* she has acted out several parts of the story while I have been working in the kitchen. On Saturday at Warrington beach she looked all around her at the toi-tois, feathery beach grasses which did look like Ukraine corn. She laid two pieces across the inside of her elbow, put her head a little on one side as she had seen in the picture, held the corn out to me and said, 'Say thank you Varya.'

Thus the foreign story is acclimatized and given a local meaning. As with Varya's book so with *Children of the North Lights,* the d'Aulaire picture book about Lappland. For all the remoteness of the story, the snow, the difference in the Lapp life from day-to-day Dunedin, there was enough similarity for Carol to feel at home. The children looked like her old friends the Eskimos: there were reindeer, sledges, school, church, babies, and a christening, all familiar enough from either the 'real' or the 'paper' world. Carol was fascinated with the Finnish vapour bath, 'bare tummies', and with the tent of the Lapp family. Some envy of this. If puzzled at moments she was curious and interested all the time. She is anxious to learn now, quite consciously: the unfamiliar is not brushed aside if she has a single clue about it. She needs some bridge-way however, some foothold. Another d'Aulaire story *Ola* was too strange for her.

[Notes of April 1950. After breakfast yesterday as I made up the kitchen fire she began, 'You said water puts fire out.' We had been talking yesterday about the burning house in *Katy and the Snow-Plough* and she has seen some magazine pictures of a fireman and his hose. 'It does put the fire out Carol.' 'But look, you know that bath book?' This meant nothing to me. 'Yes, the bath book, the very very snowy book.' I then recollected the d'Aulaire story, and she went on, 'They put water on the fire in the bath and it was still hot.' I knew where I was and I had an absorbed listener to an impromptu lecture on the Finnish vapour bath.

Children of the Northern Lights, like *Mei Li*, was only read to her a couple of times but the two books extended her experience in an immeasurable way. At odd times for months one has seen her adding bits on to those frameworks in her imagination. They seem to have illumined her world, *Mei Li* particularly—that book has given her a companionship during these solitary months when she has been entirely without playmates.]

6 FEBRUARY 1950

We have been reading more poetry together. Dick has been reading *A Child's Garden of Verses* to her at night for about a month, and I have been choosing poems from Michael Williams's *Modern Verse for Little Children*. Her favourites are Humbert Wolfe's *Blackbird*, *The Rain* by W. H. Davies, *Someone*, *The Cupboard* and *Bread and Cherries* by de la Mare, Rose Fyleman's *Fairy Went A-Marketing* and Emile Jacot's *Jack Tar*. Edith Sitwell's *King of China's Daughter* puzzled her. There were just too many things to explain in this. She found the whole idea of 'not loving' quite disturbing.

When I read the favourites she doesn't look at the book; she looks outward, and you can almost see her watching pictures. The poems she likes contain nouns that she is familiar with. Any old adjective will do, even a verb, but the nouns must be known.

Today I read twice *The Three Bears* by Robert Southey. This is the original story as Southey told it in *The Doctor*, Volume 4, Chapter 129—the first version with a lovely eighteenth century style of telling: 'for they were good bears, a little rough or so, as the manner of bears is, but for all that very good-natured and hospitable.' And this: 'So she seated herself in it, and there she sat till the bottom of the chair came out, and down came hers, plump upon the ground.' The text is hand lettered in two colours, and the look of the print is as good as the substance of it.

I was telling Dick about how much Carol likes this version of *The Three Bears,* and he said he could never understand how the author of the *Lives of the British Admirals* happened to have this odd brain-child. Nor can I.

[A week or so after this I borrowed Jack Simmons's *Life of Southey,* which made the whole story quite clear. Southey, who spent much of his childhood at the house of a maiden aunt, had like Beatrix Potter one of those solitary repressed childhoods which he was later to describe in a letter thus: 'I had no playmates . . . if my aunt was writing letters I was to sit silent. There was a garden but in playing there my clothes might be soiled.' The lonely child beguiled the time by playing with his fingers and fancying pictures in the curtains. It might have cramped a man for ever, but like Beatrix Potter he survived. Ever afterwards, as father or uncle or friend, he was to be on the side of children. Certainly in his life there were some compensations, as Simmons makes clear. 'One of his aunt's friends had married the son of John Newbery, the publisher of *Goody Two-Shoes* and the rest of those delightful eighteenth century children's books—"radiant with gold and rich with bad pictures" as Leigh Hunt called them— and in due course the boy was presented with them all.'

Southey was therefore a child in touch with the best children's literature that his time could provide. His aunt, too, was passionately devoted to the theatre, and the young Robert saw his first play at the age of four.

His greatest treat was to go to his grandmother's at Bed-minster, for that was really in the country and there he might play in the garden and get dirty 'the very paradise of my childhood' as he called it sixty years later. The house was Georgian built by his grandfather about 1740. Its porch was covered with jessamine inside and out: it had a flagged hall, giving access to the best parlour on the right and the 'best kitchen' in which the family lived on the left. This was a 'cheerful room, with an air of country comfort about it', stone-floored, wainscoted, furnished with cherry-wood chairs and tables, its walls hung with old maps and mirrors in white frames. Over the parlour was the green room occupied by Edward Tyler: over the best kitchen was the yellow room, for visitors; and above the other kitchen was the blue room, belonging to the old lady herself. On the back of the house was a fruitful vine. Behind it lay the barton with an outhouse containing dairy, laundry and stables, almost completely covered with clipped yew. Here too there was an orchard, and one of those charming kitchen gardens where flowers and vegetables grow together bounded by a wall on which cherries, peaches and nectarines climbed.*

This is the world Ruth Lippiatt recreates in her illustrations to *The Three Bears*. Here were happy days to Robert Southey, who grew to be a good father if not a major poet. When he married he went to live at Greta Hall, where in the course of time he came to resemble an island almost entirely sur-rounded by children, his own supplemented by those of Coleridge, whose wife was Southey's sister-in-law. Much of the hack-work which Southey did—*Lives of the Admirals* for instance—was written to keep these children fed and clothed. Once one knows the story there is no riddle about the author-ship of *The Three Bears*.

It must be two months since Carol had *Mei Li*, but yester-

*J. Simmons. *Southey* (Collins, 1945), p. 12.

day the story was much on her mind, particularly M.'s kitchen, the beggar girl, and the brother.

C: We are talking about China now. You're Mei Li and I'm her mother. Now, Mei Li, what would you like for dinner?

28 FEBRUARY 1950

The week of 18 to 25 February was spent at the beach. We haven't been away on a holiday together for eighteen months, so this was a big experience for Carol—not only the beach, with all the gulls, even a penguin, but the packing before we left, the journey out, and her sudden pangs of concern for father's welfare while we were away. Also the slightly painful adjustment to the number of rules in someone else's house. There were so many things she must not do. But if the house itself was a greater constriction, the beach was a freedom wider than anything she has ever known. She is quite fearless of wave and water. Even a near-drowning accident which came to her ears did not make her fearful in any way.

She saw all the sheep and cows and horses she misses in town; at times I felt there was rather a plethora of cow when we rowed up the river one day, three adults, two babies, and Carol. The herd of Jerseys wading across the stream from one paddock to another seemed grimly close to me, but Carol was ecstatic. She pointed up the bank, 'Look at the cows, hundred of cows!' Then a grin, 'Millions of cows.' Then she saw a homestead in the distance. 'Is that Farmer Jones' house?' I agreed it was, to lend her more enchantment to the view, as though that were necessary. 'Can we go and see him?'

Her vocabulary at the moment is growing fast, as she picks up words such as actually, decided, complicated, possibly, probably, separately. I notice, however, that with some words the initial consonant does not register. Hence the earlier muddling of 'cush' and 'thrush', 'Eric' and 'Derek', 'christen' and 'prison'. 'If he is naughty he will go to christen.' All this makes an odd mixture in her talk, the confetti of adult words mixed with the curious vividness of childhood's language, as when she banged her finger and it festered. 'It's boiling.'

5 MARCH 1950

The Story About Ping by Marjorie Flack and Kurt Wiese, Dick has already read twice to Carol. Ping is a duck who lives with mother, father, two sisters and three brothers, eleven aunts and seven uncles and forty-two cousins and the master of them all, on a houseboat on the Yangtse River. Each morning the ducks march over a narrow plank from the boat to the shore, where they hunt for snails and fishes; and each evening they return home. The last duck home is flicked on the back. One night, being late and fearful of punishment, Ping does not return to the boat and he is left behind. He swims down the river next day in search of his family, but meets instead with misadventure and capture before he finally reaches safety.

The background of the story is foreign and strange, but the four-year-old seems excited by things because they are strange. In contrast to the two-year-old who is most interested in what is most familiar, four years responds most to what is less familiar. One can read a story about remote places now to Carol as long as the pictures make the reality quite clear. The illustrations must still confirm the text; the two together, words and pictures, can take the child far beyond her immediate experience. In this story of river life in China, Carol was entranced by pictures of fishing cormorants and interested in the rings about their necks which prevent them from swallowing the catch. She saw the point of the barrel tied to the child's back to save him from drowning should he fall into the river. All this is related to her practical interest in how and why.

The four-year-old interest is met, too, by the numbering, which is at the poetic level not the strictly mathematical. Three brothers, eleven aunts, forty-two cousins—proper counting doesn't come into this verbal play with figures any more than it does in 'millions of cats'. Carol talks about numbers and counting in exactly this way. 'How old is Mr Procter? Sixty-forty?' Or when we play shops and I ask the price she tells me: 'Six and fivepence, two shillings. No, it's 65.'

We have read *Polly and Jane's Houses* again. She still likes the details of leaves and flowers for cups and saucers. Her own play outside follows fairly closely along the lines of this story.

Three days ago I read her Robert Bright's *Georgie*. As a librarian I would have criticized this ghost story as over sophisticated in theme; as a parent with a child I found no fault. 'Up in the attic of this little house there lived a little ghost and his name was Georgie. Every night at the same time he gave the loose board on the stairs a little creak and the parlour door a little squeak and then Mr and Mrs Whitaker knew it was time to go to bed, and Herman the cat knew it was time to prowl and . . . Miss Oliver the owl knew it was time to wake up and say "Whoo-oo-oo".'

Then the board is mended and the door oiled and the little ghost sadly seeks another house to haunt. Even a ghost in the straitened nowadays may have housing difficulties. Georgie stays in a cow barn until wind and weather at Mr and Mrs Whitaker's produce again a creaking board and a squeaking stair.

Carol of course asked 'What's a ghost?' I pointed at the

picture of Georgie and said, 'That is.' She can accept croco-
diles under similar circumstances, and ghosts presented no
problems. I was amused next day to find her with a piece of
elastic fallen into a shape on the floor. 'Look Mummy,
Georgie.' As the word ghost has no evil connotation for her
she thoroughly enjoyed this story.

I have read her *The Three Bears* again—still very popular.

15 MARCH 1950

Carol and Helen saw the pantomime *Mother Goose* on Saturday afternoon. We let her understand that this was a children's
opera, because she had been so envious a year ago when we
went off to *Rigoletto* and *Aida*. We went dressed up in our
finest, Carol in party dress and pink hair-ribbon, rather like
a box of chocolates. When we were at the theatre she did
not follow the actual plot—who could? but the spectacle was
all: demon king, a ghost, fairies dancing, a golden palace with
golden chairs. She pointed out that the Principal Boy was a
girl, and she had similar difficulty with the sex of the dame.
A slapstick interlude with pastry in Mother Goose's kitchen
was the great scene to her. In the children's theatre 'business
is all', as A. A. Milne has remarked.

[March 1951. In a story she was telling me about herself as
a queen the pantomime has left its mark twelve months afterwards. 'I live in a real palace with golden roof and golden
chairs and golden curtain and I have nineteen babies. Jack's
the king.' Jack is her imaginary husband of some months'
standing. He is a mixture of Jack C. and Jack M.]

22 MARCH 1950

M. has been telling Carol a great deal about fairies. People
introduce fairies, giants, Jack Frost, and wolves to children

F

in an effort to amuse, but they leave mother to cope for months on end with the newcomer to the child's imaginative world. Sometimes I am irritated because those fears that Carol has nearly all revolve round such things as wolves and giants and head-chopping, casually mentioned in front of her and never forgotten.

We continue to have long elaborate conversations about God, death, angels, and Jesus. Carol has found *Prayers for Little Children* again.

26 MARCH 1950

Today as I stood by the stove stirring a sauce Carol said, 'Tell me some poems.' So I recited as I stirred, *John had great big waterproof boots on, Double double toil and trouble, Dr Fell, Someone came knocking,* and one or two others, until my memory for 'suitable poetry' completely failed. 'More,' the demanding voice kept saying. So I went on to

> *When as the rye reach to the chin*
> *And chopcherry, chopcherry ripe within*
> *Strawberries swimming in the cream*
> *And schoolboys swimming in the stream,*
> *Then, O, then, O, then, O, my true love said*
> *Till that time come again*
> *She could not live a maid.*

'Chopcherry, chopcherry,' Carol chanted. 'More!' So I recited *Daffodils* and the *Ode to a Grecian urn.* 'That's a long one. More!' However by now the sauce was done and the rest of the dish required all my thought.

I had the impression as I spoke that Carol would have listened to absolutely anything I said even if it had been poetry in a foreign language. It's as if she does a special kind of listening when you fix your eye on her in ancient-mariner style. Certainly it's a different kind of attention from that which she gives me when I read to her. There is a wide gulf that lies between reciting or telling aloud and reading, like the gulf between reading to one child and reading to fifty.

28 MARCH 1950

Complaints that she hasn't had any new books for a long time. This morning I went to the library and returned with half a dozen.

Carol spent an exceptionally quiet hour in her room looking through them all before she settled on what I should read to her. The lot fell upon Edward Ardizzone's *Little Tim and the Brave Sea-Captain*. I have seen this described as a 'mock serious' tale—serious yes; mock, no. Carol found it a straight adventure, indeed a quite terrific adventure in the latter stages of the story. Real danger, not a parody of it.

One morning the wind started to blow hard and the sea became rough, which made the steamer rock like anything . . . all that day the wind blew harder and harder and the sea got rougher till by nightfall it was blowing a terrible gale. In the middle of the night there was a fearful crash. The ship had struck a rock!

(Conrad in the kindergarten.) I read at a slow pace and Carol's face a solemn stillness holds. The pictures are dark and fearsome but quite explicit: most ingeniously they are tipped this way and that, awry to show the effect of the rocking storm. Then, just soon enough, relief comes—behold the life-boats! With the slackening of the story's tension Carol resumes her Socratic role.

From the moment I began the story there were questions, firstly the simple demands for a definition, always prominent in the first reading of any book. 'What's a galley?' 'What's a Cunarder?' or 'What's grog?' 'A special drink sailors like,' I say. This proves acceptable to her, and she adds 'A bit like lemonade.' These are routine questions not usually repeated once she has the information she seeks. There is a second type of question, however in which she tries to square a book with

her own experience. These questions, I've noticed, may recur over many readings, and in an extreme case she may even refuse to accept the book version. Gradually I have learned to take most pains with these queries, to answer them as thoroughly as I can.

In the beginning of the story Tim and his sailor friend

row from the shore to a liner anchored out in the stream. This is immediately questioned. She wants to know why the ship doesn't come up to the wharves as she has seen the overseas vessels do in Dunedin. I embark on a discussion of harbour depths and she is perfectly satisfied that Tim's harbour compares unfavourably with the port of Otago. All this fits in nicely with her view that whatever is local is best. One point I did not satisfy her about. The sailor leaves Tim behind: he forgets his passenger. Carol was very sceptical about this and I longed to say, 'Because of the plot dear because of the plot!'

Stranded on the liner, Tim as a stowaway, albeit an accidental one, gets the traditional treatment meted out to such. He is set to work scrubbing until his back aches and his fingers grow sore. Carol was again puzzled: she enjoys scrubbing, one of her favourite indoor sports. I have to elaborate on the area of decks and the quantities of dirt on them. She nods thoughtfully, as the idea gets through to her that scrubbing may not be under all circumstances, one of the finest experiences of life.

Tim is rapidly promoted, for he has all the virtues and the luck of the fiction hero at sea. He is allowed to assist in the galley, and 'besides helping cook he would run errands and do all sorts of odd jobs such as taking the captain his dinner and the second mate his grog, helping the man at the wheel and sewing buttons on the sailors' trousers.' A very delirium of happiness in fact—the buttons were the climax. Carol, currently in the middle of a sewing-bee, examines this picture closely.

With all the pictures there is this same careful eye watching out for every detail. She sees far more than I, to whom small, in a picture at least, may spell unimportant. Thus one night Tim, after his manifold activities, climbs into his bunk 'so tired he didn't even take off his clothes'. Carol enquires, 'Did he keep his shoes on too?'

'Oh, yes.'

'No, he didn't.' She points to a corner of the picture—shoes, about a quarter of an inch of shoe.

I should perhaps record a third class of questions, the traps for an unwary parent.

[Ever after this, whenever Carol and Dick went down to the wharves on Sunday she asked to be shown the ship's galley. Galley visiting in fact became part of the Sunday routine.]

After this we read L. Leslie Brooke's *The Man in the Moon*.

29 MARCH 1950

Today we read Ludwig Bemelmans' *Madeline* together. Immediately it was finished she asked for the story again. On the first reading the couplets in which Bemelmans tells his story each required a longish exegesis—in fact there was more exposition from me than text from him.

> *In an old house in Paris all covered with vines*
> *Lived ten little girls in two straight lines.*

Simple, but 'What's Paris?' 'What are vines?' Paris first. I tell her it is the big town in France, as London is the big town in England. France, which is a new country to Carol, I describe as a country near England; thus it now has an identity and a proper projection on her map of the world. Vines next. 'Like our wisteria on the front porch'. I am ready to tackle the subject of boarding-schools and the two straight lines. She often sees the Columba College girls on Saturday afternoons going by in a crocodile, so the straight lines of walks and dormitories and school meals, all an important part of *Madeline,* can be related to something she knows. But there is still a remaining 'Why?' 'Why are the little girls sleeping at school? Why aren't they with their mummies and daddies?'

As Madeline and her schoolfellows walk through Paris Carol was enchanted with Bemelmans' pictures—of churches, and gardens, and balloon sellers. She was delighted also when Madeline 'said "Pooh" to the tigers at the zoo', but all paled before the glory of Madeline's 'appendicitis' ('Is that like measles?') and the midnight rush to hospital in an ambulance with a red light. Dr B. had described hospital in glowing colours to her some months ago when it seemed probable she would have to go there herself. The hospital of the story confirmed all his rosy description. Madeline sitting up in bed, surrounded by presents and admiring schoolfellows, with a scar on her stomach and a basket of flowers, seemed a heroine in luck.

She loved the end printed in small type:

And she turned out the light—
And closed the door—
And that's all there is
There isn't any more.

30 MARCH 1950

When we were talking about the way Carol's fears were quietened by comparing the darkness to the sleepy book Pat, who was here last night, told me of a rather similar incident when her son was disturbed by an electric meter near his room which made a curiously alarming noise on frosty nights. She was about to move the child to another room when she happened to read him one of Madeline Nightingale's poems in which this line occurs: 'I heard the darkness singing to itself.' 'Just like my room,' he said, and minded the noise no more.

31 MARCH 1950

While I have been working in the kitchen today Carol has been looking at Theodore Seuss Geisel's *And To Think That I Saw It on Mulberry Street* and Maud and Miska Petersham's *The Christ Child*. I was much too busy to sit down and read, but she came beside me at the bench, turned over pictures, and I talked them over with her.

I looked back to *About Books for Children* to see what I had written about *Mulberry Street* there.

A small boy who is usually catechized by his parents regarding what he has seen on the way home, sees a horse and a cart on Mulberry Street, a fact he feels is barely worth chronicling. Naturally be begins to embroider, changing the horse to a zebra, the cart to a chariot, the zebra to a reindeer, the chariot to a sled, until the final double-spread of the book is cluttered with a gaudy fantastic picture of a magnificent procession with the town band, a corps of cycling policemen, aeroplanes, rajahs etc. It is a crazy story with this to be said in its favour, that this imaginative extension and development of a simple incident into something rich and strange is a not unusual mental process. To children this book is just funny, to the adult psychologically correct.

Well, how right I was. I even feel slightly irritated with that other non-maternal self for hitting the nail on the head. Once one has children one dismisses all one's prenatal opinion as so much dross.

I told Carol that the story was a boy's 'pretend'. She looked at all the pictures with a grin something like the one she wears for *Bad Mousie*.

Then she took up *The Christ Child* and came to me with the book open at the Roman legionary reading from his parchment to the populace. 'And it came to pass in those days that there went out a decree from Caesar Augustus, that all the world should be taxed.' I told her that a long time ago when there were no newspapers and no telephones, and the king wanted to tell his people something he sent one of his soldiers and wrote what he had to say in a book. 'Mummy, that's not a book,' she said, pointing at the scroll. 'That's what they used to have as a book Carol,' and I rolled up some fools-cap as a scroll for her to play with. As I worked I told her about the king or emperor (a special kind of king) whose name was Caesar Augustus, how he needed some money and wanted taxes (money for the king); how everybody went to his own city which meant the town where he was born, and how when Joseph and Mary went to Bethlehem all the hotels were so filled with people that they had to sleep in a stable. The picture of a baby among the straw upset her, the animals were so close.

C: Would they bite?
D: No they wouldn't bite that Baby.
C: They'd just come close and give Him a kiss.

How much of this explanation sinks in I don't know. I overheard her talking to the Bermot doll about the picture of 'All went to be taxed, everyone to his city.' She said, 'Bermot doll, this is the circus at God's place.'

Her other play today was an attempt to make trousers. She is usually busy with dolls' dresses, but *Little Tim* has left his dent on her consciousness.

3 APRIL 1950

Last night Jean came round for Sunday supper. As a privilege Carol sat up with the grown-ups to practise 'being quiet when visitors are here'. Fair success only. Jean has quite recently been in Paris and in London where she attended the

Buckingham Palace Garden Party. Carol sat still like an aco-
lyte, listening to a description of the Royal Family and the
clothes they had worn. Then the palace—about the kitchen
—Jean had to admit she hadn't seen that. 'Did the Queen get
the tea?' said Carol. I was reminded of E. Nesbit's stories
about the homelier side of palace life.

While I, no queen, prepared the meal, Jean read Carol
Madeline. I didn't hear all the reading, but I overheard Jean
chatting in asides about the gargoyles on Notre Dame and
the fountains in the gardens, giving her a child's eye view of
Paris which was delightful.

'Do you know what I say to tigers at the zoo—"pooh",'
said Carol.

Today she has been playing kings and queens all day. There
is a mixture of blocks arranged on top of the toy chest. 'That's
the palace, see, all shiny,' she says pointing at the light falling
on sharp green edges. After lunch she unearthed paper hats
and wanted me to play royalty while I washed dishes. I wasn't
having that—*lèse majesté* from father's point of view. When
I told Dick he said, 'Republics miss a lot of fun.'

4 APRIL 1950

Today a letter came from Joyce on S.S. *Tamaroa*. I read
an adapted version to Carol who had been highly delighted
to receive a postcard from Lenore a week or so ago showing
her ship.

C: 'What a lot of people we know all going to England
where Auntie Sheila lives—Joycey, Lenore and Miss Hollis,
and Rohan—but we only know one that's seen the King.'
Then a look of sudden consternation. 'The rock—what about
Joyce's boat and the rock?' (Little Tim again.)

'Joyce won't go on a rock,' I assure her. We go into a

long conversation about rocks at sea—why you don't see them, darkness at sea, lighthouses and where to put them, where the moon was if it was so dark.

C: 'I can't see the moon when it's raining and the trees all windy. The *engineer* should have *seen* the rock.' I repeat my assurances that Joyce won't be shipwrecked, yet she is not entirely convinced.

7 APRIL 1950

Snow yesterday. The stocks and poppies in the front garden looked ridiculous islands of colour. I have never seen such a mixture of seasons—trees over the road just turning yellow, in a routine autumn way, summer flowers, and all of it entirely surrounded by snow. Carol, full of memories of the light fall last winter, was anxious to be outside to make a snowman which she capped with her old red beret.

We had a long involved conversation in the afternoon by the fire, on the subject of swaddling clothes. How it came up I don't remember. Oh yes, she was dressing up a black doll in an old bandage and looked up to ask, 'What does that look like?' 'It looks like a papoose to me,' I said, for we have been singing *I'm an Indian too* from *Annie Get Your Gun*, 'or like Baby Jesus in swaddling clothes.' 'What are swaddling clothes?' 'That's the way they used to dress babies a long time ago.' 'Before I was born?' 'Before you were born and before I was born and before your Nana was born and before her mother was born.' 'And before Daddy was born?' 'Yes, before Daddy was born.' 'And have all the mummies with swaddling clothes thrown them away?' 'Well there are some in museums.' 'I've never seen them in *my* museum.' 'No, I don't think there are any there, but in the very big museums in Paris and London they have some swaddling clothes.'

I am on touchy ground. For some time now Carol has
insisted that what she has is biggest and best. I think that it
may be useful to explain, while on what I imagine to be the
neutral ground of museums, that it is possible for something
to be bigger elsewhere. So I stick to my guns; the British
Museum is bigger than the Otago Museum. Carol is seriously
displeased, and her eyes wander round the room. She begins
to talk about Pamela, an English cousin whom she has never
seen. When I won't shift from my position on the museum
question, she asks, 'How big is Pamela?' 'Fourteen.' 'How
much is fourteen?' I show her. 'She'll be too big for me to
play with. I don't want to play with her. And I don't want
to talk any more about museums.' She was obviously upset
and turned away from me back to the doll.

Twenty minutes later we fell into conversation about the
moon, and unfortunately when I began to talk about great
distances, a long, long way away, and about suns we have
never seen, again I felt the tension rising. 'We won't go on
talking about this any more,' she said, and once more picked
up the black doll. One could feel the thrusting away of facts
which were unpleasant.

Tonight in bed I thought she needed some comfort after
the impact of disturbing ideas in the afternoon, so I read her
The Christ Child. This was one of my first loves among
American picture books, indeed this and *Mei Li* I think are
my favourites still. *The Christ Child* is one of relatively few
religious books for children which do not nauseate one with
sentimentality. So often in a chase after appeal to childhood
the producers of such books throw dignity to the winds; not
the Petershams. They have used as their text the Authorized
Version and made for their illustrations coloured lithographs
which have a grave charm. I can't help comparing their soft

gentle pictures with the merely sugary ones of *Prayers for Little Children*. The point is, possibly, that of the two, only the Petersham book was made in a religious spirit; certainly the laborious lithographic process would only be used by artists who cared with a religious intensity about what they were making.

I was about to begin on the second page of the text, where the angel comes to Mary, but Carol would have none of this. We had to begin at the beginning, where Isaiah's prophecy is quoted. I explained what a prophecy was and I read:

For unto us a child is born, unto us a son is given; and the government shall be upon his shoulders; and his name shall be called Wonderful, Counsellor, the Mighty God, the Everlasting Father, the Prince of Peace.

On this first actual reading (for we have only talked about the pictures before) I did adapt the text slightly to her understanding. As soon as possible it will be read as written, but I want her to understand what it means first of all. When we came to the pictures where the text reads, 'And it came to pass in those days that there went out a decree from Caesar Augustus, that all the world should be taxed. And all went to be taxed each to his own city', it was obvious that she understood this. Last week's explanations had meant something after all. There were no questions as in the earlier pages, and the slightly strained look relaxed. She was surprised that no angels were drawn 'in the flesh'—does one use that expression of angels?

When we came to Mary 'great with child' I elaborated, and she stroked the picture of Mary on the donkey at a probable curve. It is interesting to notice that Joseph in this picture is a traditional, slightly Othello-looking figure, like the Joseph of the Cherry Tree carol. Any distress over the picture of the manger surrounded by animals has gone. She adores this now in quite the precise dictionary sense of the word, 'to regard with the utmost respect and affection.' The operative word is 'affection'.

About the shepherds abiding in the field there was some argument. She could not believe they were men, because of their robes, and even when I thought I had her convinced she clutched as it were at a very small shepherd. 'That is a little girl.' [She persisted with this belief for months afterwards.] I skipped over Herod's temple and moved on to the Wise Men. This is one of the Petershams' most perfect and childlike pictures. I rather bungled the Herod business. Carol sensed that he was a figure of fear. Most of all she liked the boyhood in the carpenter's shop. 'What is He making?' Very interested in Jesus at the temple 'having conversations and asking questions'— to Carol the most rational activity. As when the boatman 'forgot little Tim' she rather questioned that Mary and Joseph would go away from the temple without their Son. She does not consider this wholly adult behaviour.

The book closes, 'And Jesus increased in Wisdom and stature, and in favour with God and man.' 'That means,' said I, 'growing bigger and knowing more things.' She patted the picture affectionately. 'I'm going to keep this book for ever and ever. And now we'll have *The Man in the Moon*'—which we did.

11 APRIL 1950

Yesterday morning very hot—the paper says 76°. Found Victoria on the porch in her play-pen where I had left her, but wrapped up in a pillowcase tied at her waist with a red hair-ribbon. When I asked Carol about this she said, 'I put Vicky in swaddling clothes.' Later in the morning as I was tidying her room, 'Well, I'd better go and see how Jesus is getting on,' she said, and out she went to see Vicky.

In the afternoon L. drove us all out to the Taieri plain and over the hills beyond. Carol, looking out the back window of the car, was excited about the colours of the landscape, early autumn grey-blue and yellow in the late afternoon. She was excited, too, about the sheep, and spent a lot of time looking for a black one. 'Mummy's woolly purse. That comes from a black sheep. Why aren't we going to see Farmer Jones?' As in February when we were at Brighton, I realized again how much the *Animals of Farmer Jones* had meant to her.

To my horror and Carol's joy there was a mouse in the kitchen this morning. 'I'm not afraid,' she boasted. The influence of *Madeline* is infectious. Then reminiscently she gave me a line from Rose Fyleman's poem, 'I like mice, they're rather nice.' We seemed to talk mice all day until I could have screamed. Her last words tonight before going to sleep were, 'Those little fieldmice Snippy and Snappy, you like *them?*'

And a lovely sentence: 'On your next birthday there are beautiful presents going to be brang.'

Tonight I have been looking back through the diary with a feeling that it can't all have happened.

13 APRIL 1950

Carol in bed all day today with a slight temperature. In the afternoon she asked me to read from the new library books. The first was Margaret Wise Brown's *Little Fisherman,* a story of two sizes, one small and the other—

a great big fisherman with big boats, and big sailors on his boats, with big ropes and big brushes and big fishnets, and a little fisherman with little sailors and little ropes. . . . They sailed over big waves and over little waves. Big birds and little birds flew over them. Big porpoises and little flying fish and seals leapt out of the water into the air beside them. They sailed and sailed till the land behind them was out of sight and only the sea and the sky were all around them—the blue sea and the blue sky.

Before I had finished with the list Carol was pointing out the seals. 'There's a mummy seal, there's a daddy seal and here's a little seal—and that one that's an auntie seal.'

I read on: 'Down below in the fishing grounds the fishes swam among the shadowy ledges of the sea.'

Here the artist shows the world of the fishing grounds both above the water-line and below it, an excellent semi-diagrammatic sequence of pictures. This is just the sort of thing which is admirably suited to Carol at present when she wants to know exactly how things work and how they are made. She could see small boats leaving the mother ship, fishermen throwing leads over to take soundings, and below the surface of the water the fish swimming into the nets anchored on the ocean floor. Being an uninformed parent on the subject of the fishing industry I also am pleased that the pictures are so explicit and clear. The only improvement on the book I could ask would be labels attached to the fish. The general term did not satisfy Carol. She wanted to know what kind of fish.

Towards the end of the story, when the fishing boats return to port, I noticed that they go back in the direction from which they have come, back towards the left-hand side of the page. It seems a minor point to praise, but there was some bother I remember with one of the Babar books where this convention was not observed and Carol was confused as a result. [See entry for 16 December 1948.]

For all the practical nature and detailed accuracy of *The Little Fisherman,* the book is nevertheless made with art. The text is as pleasantly rhythmical and satisfying as that 'sleepy book', the first of Margaret Wise Brown's stories which we read together two years ago—the sentences have the same pleasant dying fall to them. And even if Carol missed the point I certainly appreciated the neat twist at the end of today's story.

The big fisherman went to his big house and his big family . . . and took off his big boots. And the little fisherman went into his little house where his little family were waiting for him to have supper. And he took off his little boots. Then the big fisherman told his big family a very little fish story, and the little fisherman told his children a great big fish story.

After this we read Kathleen Hale's *Orlando the Marmalade Cat Keeps a Dog*. Carol found this full of hilarious jokes. I found jokes in it too but they were quite different ones from hers. Probably this accounts for the immense popularity of these books: child and adult both find amusement in them, but contrapuntally as it were. I have nothing at all against some jokes for adults in children's books—they have a place there, like an adult's afternoon tea on the sidelines at a children's party—although I still object to children's books in which all the fun is for grown-up people.

In Kathleen Hale's story, Orlando the cat decides to give his kittens a pet to play with. He 'suggested several kinds of animals but the kittens could not agree.'

' "What about a baby boy?" said Grace.

' "No boys thank you," objected Blanche and Patsy hastily.'

Carol hooted with laughter at this. 'No boys here thank you,' she repeated. [She used to repeat this over in the days that followed, and it became a family catchword like, 'I want to be in the middle of the join of the cuddle.']

' "I'd like a kangaroo," Tinkle decided. "I'll use its pouch to mix cement in and when I've finished the girls can use it as a work basket." '

Carol again laughs wildly.

Orlando asks his master to type out an advertisement for a pet. One of the kittens says, 'Oo, I wish I had a typewriter!' 'Do stop wanting things all the time,' he is told.

Carol laughs again but it is not laughter at an extravagance like the kangaroo-cement business or burning a mouth with cold pease porridge. This is laughter crying 'touché', because Orlando's reply to his demanding kitten is exactly what I say to Carol when her demands overpower me.

In response to the advertisement all manner of animals call at Orlando's house, kangaroo, ostrich, elephant, fox, hippopotamus. It is as though all the animal books of childhood cram into Kathleen Hale's pages, which take on here the character of a cheerful nightmare or the visions of an intoxicated zoologist.

Finally a poodle is chosen for the kittens, a brash type, rather a bounder in fact, who becomes in the end something of a 'fancy man' for mother. This is a delicious reversal of the traditional theme of adult novels where the governess is nice to father. I read in *Junior Bookshelf* of March 1947 that Kathleen Hale is a woman with a family and no help—and I should have guessed just that from this story. There is in this sketch of the mother's relations with the poodle a genuine understanding of a woman's enjoyment in having a day out.

'She enjoyed herself all right,' mutters the poodle after such an excursion. 'She likes a bit of sport and she doesn't get much round here that I can see.' I enjoyed myself all right too. It meant nothing to Carol of course but she already had plenty on her plate.

There is a rampant imagination at work in these Orlando books, bubbling up. One can almost see it happening like the bubbles rising in a glass of one of Carol's fizzy drinks. I liked

Joyce Cary's *The Horse's Mouth* for the same reason, and *The Hobbit*—Dickens too for that matter, with the 'profuse overflowing quality' which Orwell has noted.*

14 APRIL 1950

Carol still in bed, but no temperature. She has been asking me about the hammocks in *The Little Fisherman*. I made one for her doll from a large pocket handkerchief.

She is asking about typewriters too, like Tinkle in *Orlando*. 'I wish I had a typewriter. Can you get toy ones? Have Molly and Polly got typewriters?' I say not. 'No Americans, not even Paris,' she says sadly. The plethora of toys in *Let's Play House*, the Molly and Polly book, had been so noticeable that I had explained to Carol some of the facts of life about the toy position in New Zealand and the United States respectively. Paris, the new country of *Madeline*, she must see as something superior even to America.

This afternoon I read her *The Three Bears* once, and *Madeline* twice. We were in the middle of *Madeline* when Clare came over to enquire about Carol, who had been missed from her observation post at the front gate. I finish the book. Carol chimes in with the pieces she remembers and gives Clare a running gloss.

Book: She was not afraid of mice. . . .
Carol: I like mice. Mummy doesn't. I think they're rather nice.
Book: To the tigers at the zoo. . . .
Carol: Madeline said 'Pooh!' I'd just say 'Pooh' to little tigers, not great big ones.

Madeline is smitten with appendicitis, and Carol now in bed herself protests volubly that if she has 'tappendix' she

*George Orwell. *Critical Essays* (London 1946), p. 48.

does not want to go to hospital. 'On her bed there was a crank.' Carol, who hasn't noticed this item of hospital equipment, asks about it, and I am led into a long discussion about hospital beds and how they work. I told her about the nursing-home when I was there with Vicky, how I had a crank on my bed.

Book: . . . A crack on the ceiling had a habit
       Of sometimes looking like a rabbit.
Carol: I've a crack on my ceiling. It looks just like a little hat.

21 APRIL 1950

Carol is well again but these illnesses leave their mark. When H. asked her to the party she replied, 'I'd like to if I'm well enough', not priggishly, but taking the realistic view of bed as a contingency not to be ignored.

We have been reading again Leslie Brooke's *Johnny Crow's Garden* and *Johnny Crow's New Garden*.

I had made a mistake months ago in giving these books to Carol when she was too young to appreciate them, when her sense of the nonsensical was undeveloped. Nonsense, after all, calls for a comparatively sophisticated taste. True fantasy is a leap off from the solid body of knowledge, and there has to be a jumping-off place. The solider the rock the springier the leap—not surprising then that *Alice in Wonderland* should be the work of a mathematician.

Carol, I imagine, has sufficient grip on reality now to depart from it cheerfully. Anyway she has now taken the Johnny Crow books to her heart. She can memorize the jingles and discovers for herself all the jokes in the accompanying pictures —the calf bumping into the pig, and the lion putting his tie round two trees.

Then the Tapir
Said: 'Can anybody caper?'
And the Turkey
Was willing but jerky,
And the Pelican said
'When I'm feeling well I can'
In Johnny Crow's garden.

This appealed to her greatly. She has been going about saying 'If I'm well I can' as a joke, which seems to me a good thing. I would never have expected Johnny Crow to have a cathartic value.

'What did the rhinoceros say Mummy?'

'Puffickly preposserous,' I reply.

Then the weasels
Caught the measles
And the swan
Said 'They'll give it to John'
And the goat
Said 'Keep them remote'
But the hare
Said 'They're better in the air'
In Johnny Crow's garden.

This afternoon when I read this it lead to a long conversation on sickness and convalescence.

The first readings of Johnny Crow were mainly explanatory. Carol is working herself into the stories bit by bit. The questions and answers about odd words like 'caper', 'jerky', 'slumberwear', are now part of her enjoyment of reading. Up till twelve months ago too much explanation took the edge off her pleasure. Now her interest in a given book is whetted, not dulled, when I make an effort to see that the vocabulary of a book is understood. I stop only when she queries something.

Jean has sent her a picture of the Queen, which has reopened the whole question of royalty. 'What's a throne?' 'A special chair for queens to sit on.' 'Where does the Queen put it? Does she wear her crown all the time? Where does she keep it?' 'In her bedroom I should think.' 'In a box over her wardrobe? Is the palace all shining? Is the roof shining? Are the beds gold? Do they have gold covers? How do you be a king? What's a prince?' She is drawing her notions of Buckingham Palace from the golden scene in the pantomime. The mania for making palaces reaches new heights.

Three days after the last reading of *The Three Bears* she asked, 'What's hostipable?' I recognized what she meant. It was an echo of this: 'They were good bears, a little rough or so as the manner of bears is, but for all that very good natured and hospitable.' This is typical of some of her questions at the present time: they seem to simmer and brew for days before the lid is taken off.

I gave her an American women's magazine for cutting out, and she found a picture of a child in a sheet playing ghosts. 'Look, Mummy, Georgie.' Reproachfully: 'You took my Georgie book back to the library.' The returning of library books is always a problem. She was especially wrath about *Mei Li* the other day. 'I want that China book, *Mei Li*. I want it back. I don't know anything about China now. I've forgotten all about it.' She had that book in December and January, but her memory span is often longer. Yesterday we were discussing when she would go to school. 'October 26,' she was told. She repeated after me 'October, October, I go to school in October—October. I used to have a Tober book didn't I?' She looked at me questioningly.

'Yes, a Toby book,' said I. This was the way we usually referred to *Toby's House*.

'A Toby book. You took it back to the library — you shouldn't have.'

I explained about other children wanting the Toby book and she seemed satisfied. Her recollections were not clear enough to provoke her to a really insistent demand for it.

As at the beginning, she is still happy when the books reflect her life, as when she found a picture of children making a snow man in *Katy and the Big Snow;* but more often than

not she now tries to make her life reflect the books. This morning for example: 'I want a mouse as a pet'. I ignored this as I've had enough mouse talk. She persisted. 'I want to be like Tinkle in the book. He kept asking for pets and his sisters said "Don't keep asking for things." ' Later she found the mattress from the pram and pulled it along the kitchen floor.

C: We'll play Mulberry. Now you say what you saw, elephants and Eskimo children.

She rushed by with the mattress trailing behind her.

D: I saw an elephant and an aeroplane and Eskimo children.
C: Now again. (She returned to her original corner, then rushed by me again in the direction of the pantry.)
D: I saw three aeroplanes, a tiger and a band, etc.

We played this about six times.

How these children's books take hold and inhabit her mind! Reading the arguments in newspapers and magazines about the effects of gangster films and books on the urban adolescent, I can't help drawing comparisons between my four-year-old and teenage youngsters at an equally impressionable stage of development. When Carol's life is quiet and uneventful without excursions to town or friends to see her, the book life seems to shape all her play and conversation. Considering the town-bred boy with few outlets for his energy, I suspect that the 'blood and guts' book must stir him to action as a young child in similar circumstances is stirred to action by nursery stories.

26 APRIL 1950

Since her waking from a nightmare the other evening, I have dropped reading and found other ways of amusing her. She has been reproachful about 'no stories for ages' and I relented this afternoon. She spread all her books on the nursery floor and chose *And To Think That I Saw It on Mulberry Street* and Edward Ardizzone's *Tim and Lucy Go to Sea*. I haven't read *Tim and Lucy* to her before but Dick has done so a couple of times. He hasn't commented on Carol's reaction, but was very definite about his own. 'They are really wonderful stories.' Father and daughter are both a couple of old salts.

We begin: 'Lucy Brown was a little girl seven years old. She lived with an old friend named Mr Grimes in his beautiful house in the country.'

'Where are the animals?' asks Carol, to whom country still registers as the territory of Farmer Jones.

Lucy meets Tim, who introduces himself: 'I am a sailor and I have been shipwrecked. I am now looking for another ship.'

On Lucy's suggestion the two children go to see the rich guardian, who obligingly offers to purchase a boat. Mrs Smawley the housekeeper, however, with fears of drowning and seasickness, does not want to go to sea. 'Stuff and nonsense,' said Mr G. 'We will look for a yacht at once.'

Carol adored 'stuff and nonsense'. She has an enjoyment of all ejaculations of this kind. I remember how she used to relish the 'Tiddly-widdly-poof' of Mrs Potter's Mr Jackson. Mr Grimes ignores his housekeeper's protests and a yacht is bought.

Tim . . . told Mr Grimes that he knew of a very good captain and a very good cook. 'Good,' said Mr Grimes, 'send them a telegram telling them to come here at once. Oh, and by the way, tell the Captain to bring some sailors with him.'

One notices in this world how the children have equal status with the adults. They are people who converse with their peers—again, too, the complete seriousness of Ardizzone's narrative. Not that humour and fun are absent—indeed there is a genial quality about the whole thing and Carol found many jokes—but the book is still serious in the sense that a child's game, or a football match, or a hostess's preparations for a gay party can be serious, when energy is concentrated towards a goal.

Mr Grimes had bought the crew dark blue jerseys with 'S.V. Evangeline' printed on them in white letters. He bought Tim and Lucy one each too. They were very proud of them and that evening Lucy and Tim and the men went for a walk in the town, partly to have a look round but chiefly to show off their beautiful new jerseys.

Here the pictures of what I presume is Portsmouth are very

beautiful. While Carol looked at Lucy holding the Captain's hand I looked at the eighteenth-century houses. This perhaps was the scene of Fanny's visit when she left Mansfield Park, there possibly the ramparts where Mrs Price liked to walk on Sunday.

Edward Ardizzone has a keen feeling for what Rebecca West once described as 'the sense of process'. *In Black Lamb and Grey Falcon* she describes a woman thus: 'G. has no sense of process. She wants the results without doing any of the work that goes with it.'* This is the exact opposite of Ardizzone's attitude. He is willing to buy his hero and heroine a steam yacht, but they must work for it. The author points out how there were

. . . decks to be scrubbed, painting to be done and provisions to be put on board. Lucy and Tim helped with the painting. The cook was busy putting his galley in order. Mr Grimes trotted about making suggestions and the Captain was busiest of all seeing that everything was done properly.

The painting by Tim and Lucy, like the mention of 'beautiful new jerseys', is exquisitely calculated to appeal to children. Carol remembered some details of Dick's reading, for when we came to page 18 she said, 'Let me read this. "The cook would tell them stories about going to sea." ' She protested too when I read that the second mate was untidy. 'He's not. He's nice, and Lucy tidied up his room.' She likes the combination of domesticity and rip-roaring adventure in Ardizzone's stories. The main adventure comes when a group of rescued sailors turns mutinous and wants to take over the ship —'a villainous looking lot'. Carol was thrilled.

After this I read her *Mulberry Street*. She insisted on having it twice. 'I love it,' she said, and I can feel her excitement as the pictures on the pages grow wilder and more fantastic. The

*Rebecca West. *Black Lamb and Grey Falcon*, Vol. 1, p. 177.

whole of this book is a 'pretend', and she grasps the situation perfectly. Her confusion arises when some pictures are 'real' and some are 'it might be'.

During her bath she asked, 'Can we have pancakes for tea? Little Black Sambo had pancakes?' We compromised on an omelette with jam, and when it was finished she began to ask some delayed questions about Tim and Lucy. 'What are crew? Are Lucy, Tim, Mr Smawley and Mr Grimes crew?' (Mr Grimes I told her was the owner.) 'Could he be an owner and a passenger?' Then, 'What does arrived mean?' 'To get to a place, or to come to a place.' She looks at me and then stares out of the window and begins to talk to herself. 'Then the visitors arrived. Knock at the door and show them in. Someone came knocking at my wee small door. And I'll go out the door and ride on an—ELEPHANT, and he grew bigger and bigger and bigger and grew into Lucy.'

A very short short-story, but three books and a poem of de la Mare's have been drawn upon as sources—if the term is not too pompous: *Too Big, Mulberry Street,* and *Mrs Tiggy-Winkle.*

28 APRIL 1950

As far as conversation is concerned, yesterday and today have been 'bachelor' and 'burglar' days. We have talked and talked about them. In his Caldecott medal acceptance speech in July 1941 Robert Lawson said, 'No one can possibly tell what tiny detail of a drawing or what seemingly trivial phrase in a story will be the spark that sets off a great flash in the mind of some child, a flash that will leave a glow there until the day he dies.'*

I don't mean that 'burglar' and 'bachelor' are necessarily great flashes, but these are things which have stuck from *Tim and Lucy Go to Sea* and *The Man in the Moon.* Carol now has a

*Horn Book Magazine, July 1945, pp. 233-8.

mania for definitions. 'What does privacy mean?', or 'harm', or 'bachelor' or 'burglar', to mention some words I've been asked about in the last forty-eight hours. Yesterday when I was doing our bedroom Carol said, 'I'll tidy up Daddy's drawers like Lucy tidied the mate's cabin. Do you like bachelors?' I admitted that I did. 'What are bachelors?' I told her X is a bachelor. The question was far from settled. As Gesell and Ilg say, children this age run a topic to the ground. Carol seized on X and pursued her questioning. We discussed at length possible reasons why X had not married—and some likely candidates for his intentions. This was wicked of me. When I told Dick he was thoroughly shocked at what he called 'fostering the reprehensible female instinct for matchmaking'. I suspect he was also alarmed at the thought of what Carol might give tongue to next time she meets X.

The burglar comes from *The Man in the Moon* in the illustrated edition of Leslie Brooke's which we borrowed. It is in an old rhyme:

> *There was a man, and he had naught*
> *And robbers came to rob him,*
> *He crept up to the chimney-pot;*
> *And then they thought they had him.*
> *But he got down on t'other side*
> *And then they could not find him;*
> *He ran fourteen miles in fifteen days,*
> *And never looked behind him.*

It is not a rhyme which stirs me to any enthusiasm, but Carol was impressed by it. Leslie Brooke's pictures aroused her interest in the first place, and she connected the verse with some dinner-table conversation about Dunedin's burglary epidemic. I explained 'robber' as 'burglar'. This has led the conversation around to what burglars take, when they operate, and whether they are likely to come to our place. I told her burglars burgle in Mornington, a comfortably remote suburb. This satisfied her. One has to find such plugs to the channel of their questions. I find myself searching for good final answers.

6

Four and a Half to Five

2 MAY 1950

THE mermaids are back. Suddenly in the bath tonight Carol began to talk about them again, after a silence on the subject for some months. She wanted to know exactly whereabouts in the sea they lived and how often they came up to sit on the rocks. There was a pause while she must have been brooding on their curious anatomy, for she raised the question of their various bodily functions. I had to admit that I did not know how the mermaids had children. Thinking that one day we might read the *Forsaken Merman* I told her something of the story as I dried and dressed her; but, as I should have foreseen, the desertion of the mer-children distressed her, even after I explained that mermaids were 'flighty' and not at all like 'real' mothers. Carol listened in silence to this gloss on the situation. Half an hour later, as we were having dinner, she told me: 'You know what happened later. The mer-mummy went back.' She had just refused to believe it.

17 MAY 1950

We have done no reading this month. I suddenly realized that winter was almost on us and began to garden hurriedly. Carol and I have been outside nearly every day gathering up weeds and rubbish. We are to have a mammoth bonfire on Saturday. The cutting of the hedge, the students' procession, another birthday party and several visitors, have left Carol with little time for reading.

Even if the reading stops, however, the conversation goes on. For me, as for any parent, there is the sheer joy of listening to a child's language before correction creeps in. I relish her past participles like 'threwn' and 'knewn', sentences like 'then a tremendous excitement happened', 'you are very forgiven', or such phrases as 'birds swinging in the sky', and 'the queen of palace'. I try to keep my patience with the eternal questions: 'What's imagine?' 'What are details?' 'A detail is something small.' Holds finger up—'Is that a detail?' 'What's encourage mean?' 'What's evidently?' She then uses it, 'Evidently it's going to be the Bermot doll's birthday on Wednesday.'

For a couple of weeks now, whenever she is sitting in bed resting after lunch or dinner, I find her with the Petershams' *Christ Child*. This is her constant companion, the chosen of all her books. I have read it to her twice only, but this has been enough to establish the book and its story in her mind. When I read it I skipped over the matter of Herod's malevolence, but nevertheless she seems aware of him as a force for evil. 'What's Bethlehem?' she asked yesterday. 'That's where Mary and Joseph went when Jesus was born.' 'And that's where that horrid king was,' came the rejoinder.

This instance of a book read but once or twice becoming a dominant book is parallelled by the popularity of *My Mother Is the Most Beautiful Woman in the World*, which figures largely in her conversation although it was last read to her in January. Although she talked about the book I was not sure that she grasped the heart of the matter until she asked me at the week-end: 'Varya's mother was really ugly?' 'Yes,' I told her, 'but she looked the prettiest mother in all the world to Varya.' Carol: 'I think my mother is the most beautiful woman in the world.' (Hardly an unmixed compliment in the circumstances.) I made this the occasion for a little moralizing. Often when she has made some pictures she will say, 'Are these the best drawings you ever sawn?' I now reply, 'Yes, better to me, but Beth thinks Ann's drawings are the best.' Carol sees the point. 'All mothers like their girl's drawings the best.'

We continue to talk about mermaids. The question, 'Could we eat mermaids?' Answer: 'No, they are half-fish, half-people.' Carol still toys with the idea of edible mermaids. 'Could we eat the fish part?' I squash that idea, and she comes again on another tack. 'Are they comfortable like that? I don't think many mer-mummies would be like that—leaving their children. That's not very good, is it?' I feel relieved when she drops the ethical problems and switches over to their domestic arrangements. 'Where do they sleep? Do they have any beds? Any chairs?'

There is a silence for a while and then, 'How are animals born?' I tell her 'Like people—in their mothers' tummies.' 'All animals?' 'Yes, I think so—except birds, they come out of eggs.' I rather expected her to doubt this but the remark fell on fertile ground. 'Ducks,' she said, 'they hatch out of eggs. Mr and Mrs Mallard in that book, they hatched eggs.'

22 MAY 1950

Last night I settled down with Francis Steegmuller's *Flaubert and Madame Bovary,* which gave me real delight, particularly this letter of Flaubert's to his niece Caroline. The grave discussion of the new doll and the enquiries after 'your other girl' reminded me irresistibly of Carol and her family, and our conversation pieces regarding their health and well-being.

My dear Liline,

Thank you for writing me such a nice letter. The spelling is better than in any of your others and the style is also good. If you sit long enough in my arm-chair, lean your elbows on my table, and hold your head in your two hands, perhaps you will end by becoming a writer.

I have with me here a lady whom I found on the boulevards and who is at present living in my study, lying indolently on a shelf of my bookcase. Her costume is excessively light, consisting merely of a piece of paper which covers her from head to foot—the poor girl's only possessions are her hair, her chemise and shoes and stockings. She is waiting impatiently for my departure, because she knows that at Croisset she will find some clothes more suited to the modesty of her sex. Please give my thanks to your other child, who was so kind as to send me her regards. I send her mine, and advise her to follow a strengthening diet, for I have lately thought her a trifle pale, and am somewhat worried as to her health.

Yesterday I was at an exhibition of pictures, and thought of you a great deal. There were many subjects which you would have recognized, thanks to your erudition, and some portraits of great men whom perhaps you know. I even saw several portraits of rabbits, and I looked in the catalogue to see if I could find the name of Monsieur Lapin of Croisset. But he was not there. Goodbye my darling. Kiss your grandmother for me.

Your uncle who loves you.*

23 MAY 1950

Once last week Carol said something about 'Rumbledy, rumbledy', and I had a clue that memories of the *Pitter Patter*

*Francis Steegmuller. *Flaubert and Madame Bovary* (London 1939), pp 351-2.

G

book had somehow filtered back into her consciousness. It is two years and two months since I first read the book to her, and it was probably read a couple of months after that. Last night after dinner as I was writing out a grocery list, she suddenly said again 'Rumbledy, rumbledy through the town.' 'Which book was that?' I asked, looking up, my pencil luckily still in hand. '*The pitter patter book*—John walked through the rain—aeroplane went flying all through the town—the rumbling and the man who was dry.'

She has brought out *Paul Alone in the World* and has begun about this again. 'Would they really leave Paul all alone?' 'It was just a dream Carol, it didn't really happen.' Carol: 'Oh, they were just under the bedclothes.'

24 MAY 1950

After the success of the two Binyon books at Christmas I tried to order the rest of the series, but they were not in stock anywhere in New Zealand. Dick had to order them from England and they arrived this week. Pleasant to be this distance from wars, but irritating to be so far from publishers. Some of the books are out of print, but we got four: *Polly and Jane, The Birthday Party, A Day at the Sea,* and *A Country Visit.*

These books, compared with their American equivalents, are quiet-looking books, like Cranford compared to Chicago. That is the immediate impression, but when one comes to look into them they are seen to have a gaiety of their own. Helen Binyon, with two colours and an ingenious use of line, spots, stripes, and cross-hatching produces an effect of considerably more colour than is there in fact. The chosen colours are concentrated where a child would see them, as a lawn, a bright jersey, a red door, or tricycle. I noticed this particularly in *The Birthday Party* which I read today. The story of

Jane's third birthday party takes in the whole of the day from the moment she wakes in her cot that morning till she waves goodbye to her cousins going home down the darkened street. The treatment is completely realistic. Before her guests arrive Jane helps her mother to blow balloons—'At least Jane wasn't much good at blowing so in the end her mother did them all.' There is the moment of looking in the mirror at her party frock and the moment of shyness when the doorbell rings, the cutting of the cake and the frightening noise of crackers. There is Polly who sits eating at the table long after all the other children have left, and there is George.

They had all eaten a great deal when Tony said to George, 'Could you put a whole bun in your mouth?'
'Of course I could', said George, and stuffed one in. Jane's mother suddenly noticed that George was choking and getting very red in the face, so she rushed to him and pulled the bun out of his mouth. They all looked frightened and Susie cried; so mother said 'Now it's time to cut the cake.' But always afterwards they remembered the party as the one where George put a whole bun in his mouth.

That to Carol was wildly funny, like the jokes in *Orlando*, and as with Kathleen Hale's story I found private jokes in *The Birthday Party*. Cousin Polly, the continuous eater, was my joy. Every children's party I've been to has a Polly.

25 MAY 1950

Polly and Jane and *A Day at the Sea*. In both these stories one notices again the Binyon flair for beginning at the beginning. *A Day at the Sea* opens with the hunt in the toy-cupboard for the buckets and spades; *Polly and Jane* has all the detail of dressing for an afternoon at the park, with the capital difficulties of getting an arm into the sleeve of a coat, of putting fingers into gloves. Here are the arguments of children among themselves, the disputes with strangers, the 'No, it's mine' or 'I saw it first', the moments of alarm when parents are lost sight of—in short a child's-eye view of the world.

In *A Day at the Sea* the children are dressing after their swim. Tony the elder brother puts Tom's vest on by mistake. Carol laughed happily over this. 'Read it again!' I had to go back and re-read the incident before we could continue. The boys join in with other children playing in the sand.

Tom thought he could dig better with one of the other children's spades, but she wouldn't let him have it and pushed him over. So Tom cried and started off by himself to find his mother. He watched some grown-ups dressing on the beach. 'Don't you know it's rude to stare,' they said.

This interested Carol as a problem in ethics. She thought it was 'rude to push'—even more rude than taking a spade. We stopped in the middle of the story to have a discussion on the matter.

The concluding incident of the story, which involves the question of deck chairs was rather beyond her. I gather from Dick these are a feature of English seaside places, but Carol and I are ignorant about chairs one pays money to sit on. This part of the book is a little too English for colonial consumption.

5 JUNE 1950

On Friday we were given a set of *School Journals*. Carol found a Chinese fairy-tale with a picture of a dragon in it, her first encounter with the species. 'What is this?' 'A dragon.' 'And what does it do?' I had been reading Tolkein's *Farmer Giles of Ham*, and Chrysophlax was fresh in my mind, so I told her about flames coming out of dragons' noses and the trampling down of farm-lands. She can bear to hear of damage to a farm, while news of damage to a town might reduce her to mournfulness. I suppose to her it has the cushioning remoteness I find in a South American earthquake or revolution. She asked whether we had dragons in New Zealand, where and when and why, and I found myself explaining about prehistoric animals. Memories of Conan Doyle's *Lost World* came in useful, I muttered of dinosaurs and ichthyosaurus until by a circuitous route we reached the subject of St George. Carol sat on her stool in a trance, eyes open, mouth open, enchanted as she was on the day some time ago when I recited reams of poetry to her. She was avid for whatever I could tell her. Times like these are moments of maximum response. There is an almost hypnotic spell over the listener.

11 JUNE 1950

One learns that it is not so much what is said to a child that counts but what is said around them. Carol, who has evidently heard us talking about the films, has been telling me about an opera the Bermot doll went to, *No Room at the End*. *Whisky Galore* she imagines is a proper name. Last night while we waited for *Much-Binding-in-the-Marsh* she talked and talked, 'real grown-up talking', during which she crosses her knees, puts on what I always think of as her 'afternoon tea' face and starts in discussing her dolls and family. I remembered only the more picturesque snatches—a Kastner fragment: 'Kangaroo was born on the 95th of May. . . . Mr Whisky Galore works at the university. . . . You know Jessie, she's got twins, Judith and Peter and Jane. . . . Not a single one of them hadn't went.'

22 JUNE 1950

Margaret M. has come to stay with us while her mother

is in hospital. Both children spent a messy but cheerful afternoon yesterday with dough and rolling pins. Carol made
cakes, but Margaret played Martha and concentrated on dump-
lings. When they asked me to read this afternoon I remembered Tom Kitten's second adventure and brought out *Samuel
Whiskers* again. This time Carol was able to understand the
story. Now that she is older the book does not make such a
long strain on her attention. They listened quite breathless,
with only an occasional question. As before, when I read 'On
baking day she determined to shut them up in the cupboard'
Carol asked 'Why?' They were both puzzled at the size of
the farmhouse chimney where Tom Kitten loses his way, and
Margaret was quite worried when Tom choked with the
smoke. In her short life she has seen her mother go to hospital
three times for long periods and the experiences have made
her an exceptionally sympathetic child. She asked once or
twice whether Tom Kitten was well again. Carol's second
'Why?' occurred when the old rat and his wife fled the
Twitchit household after their attack on Tom. 'Why are they
going away?' For her it did not follow that flight was the
next and logical step.

At this point in the text there is a change from an impersonal
narrator into the first person. 'And when I was going to the
post . . . I saw Mr Samuel Whiskers and his wife on the
run with big bundles on a little wheelbarrow.' 'You didn't
see that,' said Margaret. 'No, but the lady who wrote this
book did.'

5 JULY 1950

I have read them Tasha Tudor's *Snow Before Christmas, My
Mother Is the Most Beautiful Woman,* and *The Mighty Hunter*
by Berta and Elmer Hader.

They had the Hader book to look at for two or three days before I had a chance to read it to them. I overheard a quarrel in which Margaret insisted that the buffalo was a camel. Although the children are good friends and play all day peaceably together in the nursery, they do have their clashes over matters of fact. Their backgrounds of personal experience and the books they know are different. It was a day or two before they could understand one another well enough to play the imaginative games of house and hospital. They still occasionally fall into 'Tis-tisn't' wrangles, where each is convinced she knows. They had such an argument about whales last week and another over a picture of a rabbit which Margaret insisted was a hare. Margaret is a country child, and her response to stories differs from Carol's. I noticed how caressingly she stroked the pictures of the wheat in *My Mother Is the Most Beautiful Woman in the World*.

When I read *The Mighty Hunter* Margaret obviously enjoyed it as Carol just as obviously did not. This is a story of an American Indian boy's first attempt at marksmanship. Little Brave Heart goes out to shoot a prairie dog, but dog suggests that he should find bigger game. Brave Heart finds a rabbit, rabbit suggests he shoot an antelope, antelope suggests he shoot a bear, and so forth. The climax is an anti-climax—Little Brave Heart is chased back to school by a bear.

Both children were silent when I finished. 'Did you like that?' 'I did,' said Margaret, her face wreathed in smiles. 'Not very much,' said Carol. 'Why?' 'Too many animals. Only one Indian and lots of animals.' Then she asked why the bear chased the little hunter. 'He wanted to eat him, Carol.' 'Can bears eat little boys?'—this rather incredulously. 'They can.' She looked reminiscent. 'He wouldn't like the taste of his shoes'—an echo of Mr Jeremy Fisher and his galoshes.

Although Carol had not enjoyed the actual reading of the story, she was happy talking it over with Margaret and with me. We chatted about the speed of antelopes, about tepees and papooses, and I told them how the Indians had lost their land. Just as a long time ago at Garfield Avenue all the children joined in games based on stories which they knew in common, so here *Mighty Hunter* gave Carol and Margaret a common experience in reading which they can act out together.

Last Saturday Ann came round to play, the first time this year, as she began school in February. In a new hat and coat, with one of her milk teeth missing, Ann seemed a more mature little person altogether than the child I remembered. The two children went off to the nursery to play, but twenty minutes later Carol came back distraught. 'Ann won't talk to me.' She turned to Ann's mother, her lip trembling and face red. 'I don't think it really is Ann.' We assured her it was, and she went reluctantly from the room. Soon, however, they were playing dressing-up and all was well.

It was her first intense experience of personal change.

31 JULY 1950

Margaret and her mother returned home on Friday evening. Carol, Vicky, and I stood at the gate and waved till the taxi was quite out of sight, then, a much reduced family still conscious of the gap we went back into the nursery and sat down by the fire.

'Let's have a story,' said Carol.

'Well, you choose.'

The books lay in a heap on the floor where for two months they had been used mainly for construction purposes. Unread and unasked for they had been mere gates of houses, train doors, hospital windows. The visitor gone, Carol turned immediately to her accustomed pursuits.

The two girls had asked for very few stories during the past weeks. All day long in the nursery, with Vicky as a happy spectator, they played long involved games of house and hospital, trains and barbers' shops. They asked for me only if Vicky cried persistently or needed changing. Carol seemed to be withdrawn from the adult life she had shared with me into a remote world of childhood. Even at meals the two children chatted together, so for this passage of time I have little idea of what she has been doing or thinking. It is a fore-taste of what life will be like when she goes to school. I was surprised to find myself almost lonely. They played less hap-pily with an adult in the room, for they turned to me to make decisions. In the end I saw them only at meals and bath-time.

So on Friday I took up *The Christ Child* again and read it almost entirely as it is printed. 'And the angel came in unto her and said, Hail, thou that are highly favoured, the Lord is with thee—blessed art thou among women. And when she saw him she was troubled at his saying.' 'Why?' asked Carol. 'She was surprised to see the angel, and so would you be.' I read on: 'And it came to pass in those days that there went out a decree from Caesar Augustus, that all the world should be taxed.' 'What's taxed?'

On the day I read the story first and for many months since, the shepherds abiding in the fields have been a subject of considerable debate. 'Why did they have to look after the sheep at night? Wouldn't they be tired next day?' I explained about turns. 'Then one would have to sleep in the day-time?'

Tonight in the bath she asked if shepherds would have showers. I told her 'only splashing ones in lakes'. Somehow this revealed the fact that shepherds don't have houses, and soon we were launched into a discussion of nomads, 'people who move their houses about', and a comparison with the Indian people of *The Mighty Hunter*.

She still insists that one of the smaller shepherds is a girl, and she has been draping herself as a shepherd with one of Vicky's sheets. Dressing-up has been a passion all this year. I found her in bed the other morning with an old lace supper-cloth over her head. 'I'm Mary.'

This time I read her all about Herod. She was tense and interested, although she couldn't understand why Herod didn't want another King. As before she was delighted with the manger picture and the scene of Christ in the carpenter's shop. 'Has he got his own hammer and nails?'

4 AUGUST 1950

My *Horn Book Magazine* came today. It included a criticism of an Ardizzone book with an illustration which Carol seized upon. 'Look, it's about Captain McFee.' I explained about the magazine article, that it was a 'mummy writing to tell other mummies about the fun they had reading the book.' 'She needn't tell us—we know,' said Carol rather haughtily. Which reminds me, before she left I heard Margaret tell her mother, 'Carol knows *everything* about ships.'

At tea tonight she asked Dick if he knew any nomads. 'Are all Indians nomads?' We said not, and told her about the pueblo peoples.

She is absorbed by the seasons at present. Spring has come early this year. The flowering shrubs she calls 'blossom trees'. Compounds like that are a very typical part of her vocabulary. She has a number of others, too: 'singing prayers' (hymns), 'chicken-meats' (poultry), 'field house' (a barn), 'concert-book' (a programme).

6 AUGUST 1950

Yesterday afternoon while Dick was at the football match

I baked. The children played on the kitchen floor, a kind of afternoon life which lapsed when Margaret was here and the children withdrew to their own room and their own world.

While Vicky tentatively walked, Carol acted and talked little drama after drama till her own pie-making turn came.

For some time she has been very enthusiastic about maps. *The Map That Came to Life* began it, and we have shown her odd maps in newspapers. So I brought out a calendar map of New Zealand. It was rolled up in a tube, and I showed her how the soldier with the proclamation in *The Christ Child* had read from his scroll, rolling down from the top and unrolling as he went. She was interested of course—there is a current gluttony for information—and she went round and round saying, 'Come and pay your taxes. Vicky, would you like to come to Bethlehem? Would nails do? Tacks are little nails.' I have had to explain a great deal about words which sound almost the same—mad and nomad, tacks and taxes.

In a conversation which occurred a little later one could see her striving towards a synthesis of *The Christ Child* and *My Mother Is the Most Beautiful Woman in the World*.

C: You said Jesus was a very special kind of baby.
D: He is.
C: More special than Vicky?
D: Well, yes, he is really. He is special to more people.
C (obviously trying to get to the nub of the situation): But Vicky is the most special baby of all in the wide world—to us, isn't she? More special to us?

And I said she was. Unsound theology, perhaps, but sound family doctrine.

21 AUGUST 1950

Since Margaret went home, Carol has turned back to me for conversation. Just now she is busy making distinctions, either unconsciously, as in this request: 'Will you real come to my pretendy house?', or consciously, as when she announces such discoveries as these, 'There's two kinds of secret, secrets like presents or secrets you don't tell anybody', or 'Two kinds of middle—middlesize and middle between something.' Other topics of conversation at the moment are fish and their eggs (with asides on the mermaid question), death, God, and the pantomime.

She continues to tell me stories. Several of these do not follow her old pattern of reblending and combining books she has read. Everyday life plays a larger part. Thus, her 'mop-

mender' story was based on two incidents, the radio mechanic's
call at the house and a visit Carol and I paid when we took
the vacuum-cleaner to the repair shop. From her mimicry I
should judge that she had both tradesmen neatly taped. Many
of her stories involve Australia, Jane's departure, and the imaginary playmate 'Jack my husband'. This one is typical. 'Bermot doll's father is working at the university in Wellington
and my husband is going to Australia and the children are
staying with their Nana.'

We went to the library on Tuesday and borrowed some
Caldecotts. The Surtees world of *Three Jovial Huntsmen* baffled
her, but she liked meeting the nursery rhymes in a new dress
in the *Hey Diddle Diddle* series, particularly the *Queen of Hearts*.
She has always enjoyed this rhyme, but I have just realized
that it colours her whole attitude to royalty. This was why
she asked Jean specifically about the kitchen of Buckingham
Palace. 'The Queen of Hearts made some tarts.' Her enthusiasm for the Royal Family owes much to her father's indoctrin-
ation but even more to Mother Goose. Her idea of palaces
is based directly on the golden scene of the pantomime she
saw in March. Since we read the Caldecotts she has had
another outbreak of interest in palaces. Designs of blocks and
silver-paper occupy her for hours, and her questions are legion.
'Aren't they all dressed up at palaces?' 'Can you sing at
palaces?' I sang her *God Save the King* as an indication, but
she was rather distressed. 'Isn't there one for the Queen?'
Barbara tells me Margaret was also distressed when she heard
the National Anthem. 'I wouldn't sing that one.'

30 AUGUST 1950

It is clear from her growing interest in letters and numbers
that Carol is ready for school. Although puzzled by the script

in one of her alphabet books she enjoys copying out letters.
K and T her favourites. She makes designs with spoons and
pencils. She had five one day and then added another. I told
her that if she divided them into two groups, she would have
two lots of three. 'If they are a long way away are they still
six?' she asked.

These spring days are warm and pleasant. Each morning
we take a ceremonial walk round the whole garden with Vicky
between us. Carol directs operations. 'These are the ranun-
culus. Now come and see the chives and cabbages.' Then
Vicky makes a bee-line for the crocuses in the bed under the
pear tree. She picks them by the handful with real delight.

We have read Binyon's *At the Seaside* again. Carol still
chuckles with laughter when the boy puts on the wrong vest.
Unlike an adult one, a children's joke never dulls with repetition.

A dead bee in her room. 'Where's the honey?' She had
worked it out, pigs make pork, bees make honey—honey a
by-product of dying.

3 SEPTEMBER 1950

Yesterday I read Carol *The Hobbit,* partly because she seems
ready for something substantial, partly because I can't wait
any longer to read the book to someone. I appreciated as
never before the full magnificence of the opening, with the
slow lead-in to the subject. It reminded me of a play in which
the lesser actors prepare the way for the hero's entrance and
whet the appetite of the audience. When I read, 'But what is
a hobbit?' I could feel Carol's tension relax. Now we were
coming to it. As when we read *Orlando,* she found jokes of
vast proportions where I saw something only mildly funny.
'Sorry! I don't want any adventures, thank you. Not today.'

Mr Baggins's reply to Gandalph sent her into gales of laughter and so did the song of the dwarfs:

> *Chip the glasses, and crack the plates!*
> *Blunt the knives and bend the forks!*
> *That's what Bilbo Baggins hates—*
> *Smash the bottles and burn the corks.*

Dick looked in as I was reading Mr Baggins on adventure. 'We are plain quiet people and have no use for adventures. Nasty disturbing uncomfortable things. Make you late for dinner. I can't think what anybody sees in them.' Dick had the grace to blush. 'Are you reading about *me?*'

Carol missed illustrations in *The Hobbit*. There was only one coloured picture to pore over.

C: Is this all true?

D: I don't know. That's what is in this book.

C: Where can we go?

D: I'm not sure where it is.

C: I think it's in Europe—all those dwarfs—they have dwarfs in Europe.

After supper tonight Carol gave us her traditional Sunday-night pantomime, complete with changes of scenery. 'I'll draw the curtains and there'll be one more pretty picture.' I find that she thought the 'balance-ay girls' made the scenery. Now she was the dame in red knickers wiping the kitchen floor with pastry, now she was the fairy queen. She remembers the whole performance of the *Mother Goose* pantomime in surprising detail. Even the orchestra was not forgotten—the hot-water jug did duty for that.

27 SEPTEMBER 1950

Looking back through the earlier pages of this diary, I have realized how comparatively little reading I have done with Carol over these past two months. There is suddenly so little opportunity. When it is fine we all spend violently active afternoons in the garden, and when it rains I catch up on my housework. With Vicky at her present stage it is not easy to read to Carol. Whereas Alan at eighteen months was a comfortably still listener when I read to the older children, Vicky is never still. The most mobile of children, she pulls at books, bounces up and down, pushes her hands in our faces. It's rather like keeping a pup. Although she plays with books on the floor and has done so for some time, one couldn't sit and talk to her about them, so that she has no real experience of listening. The garden is a happier solution all round.

Carol is now beginning to ask about 'true' and 'not true' stories. This is a new development. Up till now everything has been accepted as 'real'. She is still a little melancholy about the loss of Janie, and continues to make stories about people going to Australia. The mother mermaid has become an archetype of bad mother: that desertion still worries her.

On Monday morning early the four of us went down town to see *Pixie Town,* the mechanical display like a Frank Cox world, in Burns Hall. 'This is family day,' said Carol, delighted that we should all be out together instead of making our expeditions piecemeal as we usually do. On the way we called at a bookshop and were shown some Peepshow Books. We were all delighted with them and Carol chose *Cinderella* as a 'family day' present. I read this to her yesterday after lunch. She had it displayed on a round tray like a revolving stage and was much delighted with the receding perspectives. She calls it her 'prince' book, because the passion for royalty is not one jot abated. She likes the prince not so much for himself alone as because he can make a princess of whomsoever he marries.

This is her latest charmed discovery. A silhouetted figure of the prince in a doorway, shadowed against a blaze of light was her favourite picture.

Queries: 'What's a ball? Do they have them in New Zealand?' 'Have I a *fairy* godmother?' 'What are lizards? pumpkins?' 'Why had she to be home by twelve?' The magic baffled her. As *Cinderella* is her first fairy story she has never come up against magic before. She has talked of nothing else all day.

30 SEPTEMBER 1950

It seems unlikely that I shall make any more entries in this diary before Carol's fifth birthday. I am planning to take the children to see their grandmother in two weeks' time, and books, even gardening, are all subordinate now to the more urgent matter of sewing. For the last month or so Carol and I both have had a sense of standing and waiting as school beckons only four weeks away. She is like someone waiting for an adventure to begin, and I feel much as I do at a railway station performing the rites of farewell to friends going off to a larger world. On the railway platform one knows, for all the protestations on both sides, that a breach in relations is about to be made. It is necessary for the travellers that they should go to Australia, or England, or Africa or wherever it is, but their gain remains a flimsy solace to those who stay behind when the train pulls out.

So this diary as a record of one child in one home is almost done. Victoria at eighteen months, continually walking round the house in an ecstasy over the discovery of her own feet, almost drunk with the joy of being vertical, is now about the age that Carol was when we first showed her books. In one sense we have finished a stage, in another we are ready to

begin all over again with the slow turning over of pages:
'There's a shoe.' 'That's a ball.'

I know enough now of pre-school children to realize that
the name 'infant school' is a misnomer. The children of three
and four whom I know are rational beings, anything less
infantile I can't imagine. I have seen their world described in
print as a timeless void, their conversation described as so
many *non-sequiturs*. There are no *non-sequiturs* — there are
always links. Once one knows the background, the conversation follows a reasonable pattern. Children of five are responsible beings, aware of right and wrong, constructive, useful.
Living with them, one finds less of nonsense in their universe
than in the adult world beyond it. Carol and her friends to
me make Sanity Fair.

Book List

This is a list of children's books mentioned for the first time in each chapter. Many of them are, of course, referred to in several chapters of the diary, but they are listed here only on their first occurrence.

CHAPTER I

George A. Adams. *First things,* a picture book in colour photography. Collins, 1943.

Dorothy Baruch. *Pitter patter.* William R. Scott, 1943.

Esther Brann. *A book for baby.* Macmillan, 1945.

Leslie Brooke. *Johnny Crow's party.* Warne, 1907.

Margaret Wise Brown. *A child's good-night book,* with colour lithographs by Jean Charlot. William R. Scott, 1943.

Jean de Brunhoff. *Babar the king,* translated from the French by Merle Haas. Methuen, 1935.

Marjorie Flack. *Angus lost.* Doubleday, 1932.

——— *Ask Mr Bear.* Macmillan, 1932.

Margaret Gilmour. *Ameliaranne at the seaside,* illus. by S. B. Pearce. Harrap, n.d.

Dorothy Kunhardt. *Pat the bunny.* Simon and Schuster, 1940.

Lois Lenski. *Let's play house.* Oxford, 1944.

Louis Slobodkin. *The friendly animals.* Vanguard, 1944.

Bob Smith, illus. *My first book.* Simon and Schuster, 1946.
(Little Golden Books.) Text prepared under supervision of
Mary Reed, formerly of Teachers' College, Columbia
University.

Feodor Rojankovsky, illus. *The tall book of Mother Goose.*
Harper, 1942.

CHAPTER 2

Margery Bianco and Gisella Loeffler. *Franzi and Gizi.* Mess-
ner, 1941.

Margaret Wise Brown. *Indoor noisy book,* illus. by Leonard
Weisgaard. William L. Scott, 1942.

Dorothy and Marguerite Bryan. *Tammy and that puppy.* Dodd
Mead, 1936.

Ingri and Edgar Parin d'Aulaire. *Don't count your chicks.*
Doubleday, 1943.

———— *Too big.* Doubleday, 1945.

Jean de Brunhoff. *Story of Babar,* translated from the French
by Merle Haas. Methuen, 1933.

Marjorie Flack. *Angus and the cat.* John Lane, 1931.

———— *Tim Tadpole and the great bull-frog.* Doubleday, 1934.

Golden MacDonald. *The little island,* illus. by Leonard Weisgaard. Doubleday, 1946.

Lois Maloy. *Toby's house.* Grosset and Dunlap, 1946.

Beatrix Potter. *The tale of Benjamin Bunny.* Warne, 1904.

———— *The tale of Peter Rabbit.* Warne, 1903.

———— *The tale of Tom Kitten.* Warne, 1907.

Tasha Tudor. *Linsey Woolsey.* Oxford, 1946.

CHAPTER 3

Helen and Margaret Binyon. *The railway journey.* Oxford, n.d.

Margaret Wise Brown. *The little fireman,* illus. by Esphyr Slo-
bodkina. William R. Scott, 1938.

Jean de Brunhoff. *Babar and his children,* translated from the
French by Merle Haas. Methuen, 1938.

Martha Dudley. *Bad Mousie,* Donica's story, written by her mother, illus. by Trientje Engelbrecht. Children's Press, 1947.

Eleanor Farjeon. *Ameliaranne's prize packet,* illus. by Susan Pearse. Harrap, n.d.

Aileen Findlay. *The northbound express,* illus. by Rona Dyer. Christchurch, New Zealand, Williamson and Jeffrey, 1944.

Marjorie Flack. *The new pet.* Doubleday, 1943.

Leah Gale. *The animals of Farmer Jones.* (Little Golden Book.) Simon and Schuster, 1942.

Kathryn and Byron Jackson. *Animal babies.* (Little Golden Book.) Simon and Schuster, 1947.

Edward Lear. *A book of Lear,* edited by R. L. Megroz. Penguin Books, 1939.

Lois Lenski. *The Little family.* Doubleday, 1932.

———— *Spring is here.* Oxford, 1945.

———— *Surprise for Davy.* Oxford, 1947.

Edith Osswald. *Toys.* (Little Golden Book.) Simon and Schuster, 1945.

A. A. Milne. *Now we are six,* illus. by E. Shepard. Methuen, 1927.

Lucy Sprague Mitchell. *Fix it please.* (Little Golden Book.) Simon and Schuster, 1947.

Beatrix Potter. *The tale of the Flopsy Bunnies.* Warne, 1909.

Diana Ross. *The story of the little red engine,* illus. by Leslie Wood. Faber, n.d.

William Scott. *This is the milk that Jack drank,* illus. by Charles Shaw. William R. Scott, 1944.

CHAPTER 4

Association for Childhood Education. *Sung under the silver umbrella,* poems for young children, illus. by Dorothy Lathrop. Macmillan, 1935.

Margaret Wise Brown. *The goodnight moon,* illus. by Clement Hurd. Harper, 1947.

———— *The sleepy little lion,* photographs by Ylla. Harvill Press, 1948.

Walter Crane. *The baby's opera,* a book of old rhymes with new dresses, engraved and printed in colours by Edmund Evans, the music by the earliest masters. Warne, [1877].

Marie Hall Ets. *In the forest.* Viking, 1944.

Aileen Findlay. *The little white gate,* illus. by Rona Dyer. Wellington, New Zealand, Progressive Publishing Society, 1944.

Nancy Freeman. *The story of the little ant,* retold from the Spanish. Dent, 1946.

Wanda Gag. *Millions of cats.* Coward McCann, 1928.

——— *Snippy and Snappy.* Coward McCann, 1931.

Lois Lenski. *The little train.* Oxford, 1946.

Connie Malvern, illus. *Nursery Songs.* (Little Golden Book.) Simon and Schuster, 1942.

A. A. Milne. *When we were very young,* illus. by E. Shepard. Methuen, 1924.

Beatrix Potter. *The tale of Benjamin Bunny.* Warne, 1904.

——— *The tale of Mrs Tiggy-winkle.* Warne, 1905.

——— *The tale of Mrs Tittle-mouse.* Warne, 1910.

Jens Sigsgaard. *Paul alone in the world,* illus. by Arne Ungermann. Oxford, 1947.

CHAPTER 5

Edward Ardizzone, *Little Tim and the brave sea-captain.* Oxford, 1936.

——— *Tim and Lucy go to sea.* Oxford, 1938.

Helen Bannerman. *The story of little Black Sambo.* Chatto and Windus, 1899.

Reyher Becker. *My mother is the most beautiful woman in the world,* a Russian folktale retold by Reyher Becker. Pictures by Ruth Gannet. Museum Press, 1946.

Ludwig Bemelmans, *Madeline.* Simon and Schuster, 1939.

Elsa Beskow. *Pelle's new suit,* translated by M. L. Woodburn. Harper, 1929, from Pelles nya clader, Stockholm, 1912.

Helen and Margaret Binyon. *Polly and Jane's houses.* Oxford, [1949.]

L. Leslie Brooke. *Johnny Crow's garden.* Warne, 1903.
———— *Johnny Crow's new garden.* Warne, 1935.
———— *The man in the moon.* Warne, n.d.
Margaret Wise Brown. *Little fisherman,* a fish story told by
M. W. Brown, illus. by David Ipcar. William R. Scott,
1945.
Virginia Lee Burton. *Katy and the big snow.* Faber, 1943.
Robert Bright. *Georgie.* Collins, 1945.
Marion Conger. *Circus time.* Pictures of Tibor Gergely. (Little
Golden Book.) Simon and Schuster, 1948.
Ingri and Edgar Parin d'Aulaire. *Children of the north lights.*
Viking, 1935.
Deverson, H. V. *The map that came to life,* drawn by Ronald
Lampitt. Oxford, 1948.
Margaret Dunningham. *Three brown bears and the manpower
man.* Hamilton, New Zealand, Paul's Book Arcade, 1945.
Marjorie Flack and Kurt Wiese. *The story about Ping.* Viking
1933.
L. Frank. *That baby,* the story of Peter and his new brother,
shown in colour photography by W. Suschitzky. Told by
L. Frank. Collins, n.d.
Theodore Seuss Geisel. *And to think that I saw it on Mulberry St.*
Country Life, 1937.
Penelope Gibbon. *Riki the Eskimo.* Oxford, 1947.
Kathleen Hale. *Orlando the marmalade cat keeps a dog.* Country
Life, n.d.
Thomas Handforth. *Mei Li.* Doubleday, 1938.
John Hartell, illus. *Over in the meadow,* an old nursery rhyme.
Harper, 1936.
Rudyard Kipling. *The elephant's child,* illus. by Feodor Rojan-
kovsky. Garden City, 1942.
Lois Lenski. *Davy's day.* Oxford, 1943.
Golden MacDonald. *The Little Island,* illus. by Leonard Weis-
gard, Garden City, Doubleday, 1946.
Robert McLoskey. *Make way for ducklings.* Viking Press, 1945.
Lucy Sprague Mitchell, I. S. Black, and J. Stanton. *The taxi
that hurried.* Pictures by Tibor Gergely, A Bank St. Book.
(Little Golden Book.) Simon and Schuster, 1946.

Clare Newbery. *Herbert the lion.* Brewer, 1931.

Maud and Miska Petersham. *The Christ Child* as told by Matthew and Luke. Doubleday, 1931.

Beatrix Potter. *Ginger and Pickles.* Warne, 1909.

—— *The tale of Jemima Puddleduck.* Warne, 1906.

—— *The tale of Mr Jeremy Fisher.* Warne, 1906.

—— *The tale of Mr Tod.* Warne, 1912.

—— *The tale of Samuel Whiskers or the roly-poly pudding.* Warne, 1908.

—— *The tale of two bad mice.* Warne, 1904.

Roland Pym, illus. *Cinderella.* Folding Books Ltd., n.d.

Robert Southey. *The three bears,* designed by Ruth Lippiatt. Oxford, 1948.

Robert Louis Stevenson. *A child's garden of verses,* illus. by Millicent Sowerby. Chatto and Windus, 1919.

Michael Williams, editor. *Modern verse for little children.* Oxford, 1939. (Chameleon series.)

CHAPTER 6

Helen and Margaret Binyon. *A country visit.* Oxford, n.d.

—— *A day at the sea.* Oxford, n.d.

—— *Polly and Jane.* Oxford, n.d.

—— *The birthday party.* Oxford, n.d.

Bertha and Elmer Hader. *The mighty hunter.* Macmillan, 1943.

J. R. R. Tolkien. *The hobbitt.* Allen and Unwin, 1937.

Tasha Tudor. *Snow before Christmas.* Oxford, 1941.